Sweet Violet, Yellow Heartsease, Wild Heartsease, Dog Violet.

The genus Violaceae embraces some five hundred species of hardy annual and perennial plants which share the common factor of a seed capsule separating into three sections before ejecting the contents. The three most familiar and treasured members of this family are the subject of this book.

Pansies, Violas and Sweet Violets

Elizabeth Farrar

With best wishes
Elizabeth Farrar
8th June 1994.

Hurst Village Publishing

HURST BERKSHIRE

MCMLXXXIX

First published by HURST VILLAGE PUBLISHING
HIGH CHIMNEYS HURST
BERKSHIRE RG10 0TH
ENGLAND
1989

Set in Plantin

Printed and bound by BARNICOTTS LIMITED
TAUNTON
ENGLAND

For all those gardeners who respond to the quiet charm of one of the most endearing families amongst our native plants.

British Library Cataloguing-in-Publication Data available.

ISBN 0 9512481 1 1

Contents

Love-in-Idleness;

Cat's Face;

Call-me-to-you;

Jack-jump-up-and-kiss-me

Herb Trinitatis;

Three-faces-under-a-hood;

and many more fond
local synonyms.

'The many names', declared the *Florist's Museum* of 1837, 'which have been given to the generally humble but highly interesting flowers which compose the genus viola, are proofs of the high estimation in which they have been held in all ages.' Pansy, a name derived from the French *Pensée*, a thought, is the name almost universally applied to the wild flower, *Viola tricolor* and, happily, is more commonly in use for the garden hybrids than the botanically correct, but less lyrical, *Viola x wittrockiana*.

The Pansy

Viola tricolor by Alexander Marshal.
Windsor Castle Royal Library. © Her Majesty The Queen.

'It is inexpensive, it is easily managed, and it is beautiful.'

James Simkins (1889).

In earlier times, when more homes were within walking distance of the countryside, it is said that the first flower children learnt to love was the Pansy or wild Heartsease.

The status of the Pansy, although frequently gathered in from the cornfields and meadows to ornament the garden, remained largely unchanged until the early years of the nineteenth century when, almost simultaneously, two gardeners, each in the employment of an aristocratic south of England household, recognised the potential of this beloved but insignificant little plant.

According to legend, Lady Mary Bennet, daughter of the fourth Earl of Tankerville, himself a 'zealous' cultivator of plants, had laid out for herself at the family's summer residence at Walton-on-Thames in Surrey, a small garden in the figure of a heart. To this she carefully transferred the Heartsease she found growing around her father's property. Meanwhile their gardener, Mr. Richardson, took to saving seed from the more remarkable blooms in Lady Mary's collection.

It was not long before this mutual hobby excited public attention: some years later James Simkins remembered their contribution when preparing his monograph on the Pansy. 'The admirers of the Heartsease are indebted to that amiable lady and the assiduous exertions of Mr. Richardson, for being the first who brought into cultivation a family of plants which has been cultivated to such an extent as that they have now become the pride of the flower garden.'

A few miles away at Iver, Mr. Thomson, gardener to Admiral Lord Gambier, had also been enticed by the potential of this humble wild flower, and was embarking on a programme of selection and hybridisation that was to earn him the title of 'Father of the Heartsease.' The sight of professional gardeners in contest over a mere flower of the fields prompted an ironical comment from the gardening press: 'It is curious to observe that many who have spent nearly all their lives in the pleasures of a garden, have only until very lately condescended to treat the poor Pansy in any other way than as a noxious weed.' [1]

Some years later Thomson recalled those early experiments: 'Lord Gambier brought me a few roots of the common yellow and white Heartsease, which he had gathered in the grounds at Iver, and requested that I would cultivate them. Always eager to please my worthy and ever-to-be-lamented master I did so, sowed the seed, and found that they improved far beyond my most sanguine expectations.' [2]

So infallible was Thomson's eye for a promising Pansy that within a few years an early favourite, not surprisingly christened Lady Gambier, with a physique 'little more symmetrical than a child's windmill', appeared as a pygmy in contrast to later hybrids.

'One of the most important and wished for events in the life of a florist', wrote Thomas Hogg, himself a florist of renown from Paddington Green in Middlesex, 'is the raising of a fine flower from seed. His joy on first beholding it is equal to that of a lord on first viewing the infant heir of his title, wealth and honours... But to fix upon an appropriate and distinguished name for his new flower, is a work of almost as much difficulty as to raise it. No vulgar or common name can, in his opinion, speak its merits or exemplify its beauties. The flower must be ennobled by the ennobling name` of King, Emperor, Hero, and very often consecrated by the sacred titles of Jupiter, Mars, Juno, Venus. The un-lettered florist, on such an occasion, is frequently obliged to consult the parson,the schoolmaster or the doctor,as high authorities, for some learned and astounding name;' [3]

Thomas Hogg.

Thomas Thomson hybridised and christened Pansies with equal facility. A Pansy 'of monstrous proportions', *Ajax*, was surpassed both in dimensions and rich colouring by *Thompson*'s *King*. Before long they were joined by *Thompson*'s *Favourite* and *Iver Hero.*

By now competition was intense. The cultivar *John Bull*, raised by Mr. Rogers at Battersea, sported a bloom of such magnificence that other florists despaired of emulating, let alone improving on it. In 1833 the Floricultural Cabinet estimated that the country was 'only in the dawn of the Viola era', predicting that Pansies would become 'a conspicuous ornament to flower gardens in general.'

But for 'the fair sex', they posed something of a dilemma: 'Several ladies have expressed a great wish to cultivate this beautiful and interesting family, if they were not so diminutive that they cannot see their beauties without inconvenience or ruining their dresses.' Fortunately a remedy was soon proposed, a raised bed which, although not looking well in the middle of a lady or gentleman's flower garden, would 'enable anyone to see the beauties of them better.' [4]

In 1835 it was reported: 'There is perhaps no instance in the annals of history of so rapid an increase among any one natural family of plants, as in that of the Pansy... such an increase furnishes a wonderful proof of the progress of floriculture throughout England.' [5] Already there were more than 400 named cultivars to tantalise and perplex the gardener.

Even so, there were complaints that the greed of florists was responsible for the loss of many promising new hybrids, plants being flowered to death instead of being conserved for propagation. Consequently a shortage of new cultivars was inciting 'jealousy and displeasure' amongst those unable to obtain them. It was, said Sinclair and Freeman, 'like grasping at the shadow and losing the substance.'

For Thomson's competitors there was little respite.

Thompson's *King*, painted in June, 1837.

'We cannot help congratulating Mr. Thompson on having raised so fine a flower, or praising his loyalty for having so named it'.

Sales to loyal subjects were further boosted when, after the accession of the young Princess, Thomson christened subsequent cultivars *Queen Victoria* and *Frogmore Beauty*.

The indefatigable Thomson continued to select and hybridise. Up to the 183O's the dark markings or blotches on the three lower petals, for many one of the most delectable features of the modern Pansy, were unknown. But Fortune remained an ally of this already prosperous grower.

'In looking one morning over a collection of heaths, which had been for some time neglected, I was struck, to use a vulgar expression, all of a heap, by seeing what appeared to me a miniature cat's face steadfastly gazing at me. It was the flower of a Heart's-ease, self-sown, and hitherto left to waste its beauty far from mortal's eye. I immediately took it up and gave it a local habitation and a name... *Madora*.' [6]

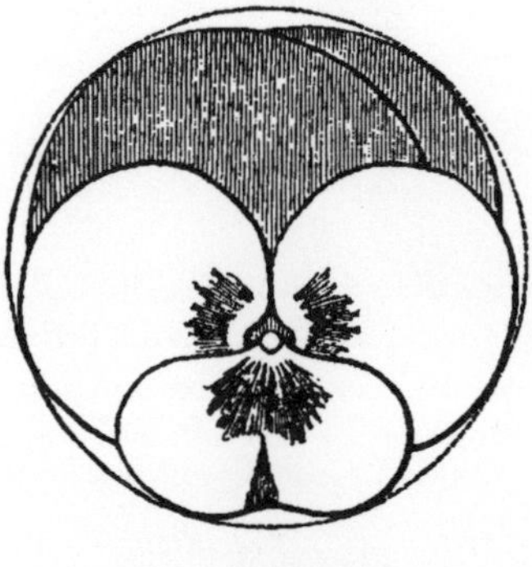

Show Pansy.

In January, 1841, the *Gardener's Chronicle* published a diagram and description of a floral novelty described as a Show Pansy: '... the first and most essential quality to examine is its form, which will be found in the greatest perfection in that flower, round which if a circle be drawn, each petal will exactly touch the circle not projecting beyond it, nor stopping short of it.'

The criteria for this most artificial of florists' flowers was to stifle the development of the Pansy for years to come.

The journey from the fragile native Heartsease, 'lengthy as a horse's head,' to the cultivated Pansy bearing large, circular, richly coloured blooms had taken nearly thirty years.

The development of the Pansy from W. Cuthbertson's *Pansies, Violas, and Violets* (1910).

The appeal of the symmetrical, regulated Pansy was such that Heartsease and Pansy societies were formed in many parts of the country.

Beeton's Book of Garden Management observed: 'It is a peculiarity of florists' flowers that they soon become subservient to the objects of the cultivator.' However there was grudging admiration for the dedicated growers who removed the blankets from their own beds for the protection of their favourite plants on frosty nights. 'Indeed the writer can vouch for one fit of gout caught in the cause.'

The reproof went unheeded: thirty years on Gertrude Jekyll complained that the Show-Pansy judge appeared to have 'no eye, or brain, or heart, but to have in their place a pair of compasses with which to describe a circle'.[7]

The improved, and improving, Pansy was at last considered worthy to congregate with tulips, auriculas and dianthus as a florist's flower; the florists, gentlemen of orderly dispositions, having finally succeeded in making the outline of the limbs more regular. (Before the 187O's the term 'florist' was applied to someone dedicated to the cultivation of a very restricted group of plants, florists competing against one another for prizes.)

By now most gardeners had become so conditioned to the silhouette of the cultivated Pansy that Jane Loudon regretted that the native Heartsease 'did not add the charm of regularity in construction to their other attractions.'[8]

> *'Nor can we enough admire that bountiful provision made by the great Author of nature, by means of which some of the most lovely blooms of the season are brought completely within the range of even the humblest cultivator.'* The Florists Museum (1837).

But the genes of the unpredictable Heartsease defied submission to a paper formula. In the early 1840's, Mr. John Salter, an amateur grower from Shepherd's Bush in West London, with a marked fondness for Pansies, removed to France, taking many of his favourite plants with him. Although the cold winters and hot summers did not suit the flowers, some four years after the family's arrival the Salter's son, Alfred, noticed some 'curious striped and blotched colours' amongst his father's seedlings. Seed was saved and accompanied the Salter's on their return to England the following year. Salter senior set up his Versailles nursery at Hammersmith, not far from their original home, and soon established 'a first rate name for many out-of-door plants.'

When first exhibited at the Horticultural Society, English florists derided Mr. Salter's wayward Pansies as 'French rubbish'.

However the three cultivars he was able to offer for sale from his Hammersmith nursery in 1851 were soon sold out, as were the sixteen cultivars sent out the following year. Unfortunately pollution in London was by now so severe that Salter was compelled to abandon cultivating Pansies; from then on experiments in hybridisation tended to be concentrated at nurseries further north, safe in the hands of such men as John Downie of crab apple fame, an authority on florists' flowers, in Edinburgh, and William Dean of Shipley in Yorkshire, who subsequently claimed the credit for coining the term 'Fancy', an appropriate label as they were indeed to many peoples' taste.

William Dean.

Now other enthusiasts in both France and England launched into the improvement and distribution of these jolly plants. 'Favoured by rich and poor alike', beds overflowed with *Alexander Grant*, dense brown blotches, upper petals bright yellow, margined and flaked crimson; *Campbell-Bannerman*, white, purple blotches, upper petals purple-edged, fine; and *David Findlay*, dark Violet blotches, upper petals claret, primrose margin.'

Flaunting its abandoned, ruffled beauty, this floral pet, blotched, flamed and edged, soon ousted the prim show Pansy from its already shaky plinth in the affections of the common gardener. Amateur visitors to flower shows were said to exhibit floral ecstasies over Fancies, which were readily obtainable from hawker's barrows.

Fancy Pansies sent out by William Dean.

But the Fancy Pansy's subjugation of the gardening masses failed to deflect the professional hybridist, lured on by the mirage of the perfect Show Pansy.

By the 189O's blotches and belting on many cultivars 'was as well defined as if they had been drawn in Chinese ink, or bronze, or purple colour by the most expert of draughtsmen.' Yet at the turn of the century 'the Show Pansy in its little box' could rely only on the florist and dedicated exhibitor to champion 'the winsome refinement' of its waning charms.

Violas

Viola allchariensis, var. *Herzogii*. by L. Snelling.

'Their hardiness and their value for spring and summer gardens, and as flowers for the house are equalled by nothing we know'. The Garden (1887).

It is said that James Grieve, best remembered for the apple named after him by his employers Messrs. Dickson & Co. of Edinburgh, was so taken with beds of Pansies that were causing a sensation at Cliveden, that in the 186O's he began to experiment with the Show Pansy, that lanky, temperamental hybrid of limited appeal to the average gardener. Selecting *Viola lutea* as the parent, a species native to the mountain grasslands of northern Britain, he 'crossed every bloom with everything he could lay his hands on' to produce the compact, floriferous and perennial plant we now know, confusingly, as the Viola, although this hybrid group is only one of many hundred members of the genus.

William Robinson attempted to clarify matters by referring to Violas and Violettas as 'tufted Pansies', waging one of his more minor campaigns in the interests of substituting homely English names for the often tortuous, and frequently rescinded, botanical classifications. On receipt of a bunch of tufted Pansies from Messrs. Dickson of Edinburgh, he blustered: 'We do not like Latin names for these varieties. They should be christened with some pretty simple name... All Pansies should have pretty names, like Ariel, not rigmarole or foreign names.' [9]

Officially, the Viola has fared little better than the Pansy, and is currently classified as *V. x williamsii*. Whatever the appropriate label, the continuing popularity of the Viola can be gauged at horticultural shows by the crowds of besotted admirers of all ages engulfing any specialist nurseryman's display.

Others went further, breeding a smaller, more compact version of the Viola, the Violetta, in form harking back to the true Heartsease of the fields. Perversely, Dr. Charles Stuart devoted ten years to eradicating the rays on the petals, reputedly a device awarded by nature as a guide to pollinating insects. Some maintained that the removal of the lines, or rays, greatly enhanced the beauty of the flower, but those regretting the loss of this curiously feline feature were recompensed by the delicious perfume of Dr. Stuart's flowers. Long after his death, staff on *The Garden* recalled the scented bunches received at their offices, 'beautiful little flowers, with the fragrance of the Violet of the field.'

In today's general catalogues distinctions are rarely made between Violas and Violettas. It is worth noting that the horn at the back of the Viola flower is an indication of perenniality and hardiness; the longer the horn, the more robust the plant.

Viola Unique: a new hybrid promoted by Cannell's nursery in 1888.

'The raising of new varieties is a labour of peculiar interest.' *The Gardener's Chronicle* (1849).

Many gardeners would regard the more monstrous of the recent hybrid Pansies as a slur on this graceful genus. Originally adapted to incline submissive petals before the onslaught of rain or heavy dew, many modern cultivars, their cumbersome physique unfitted to this practical tradition, emerge from storms as dishevelled as unpressed laundry. Happily, amongst commercial hybridisers there is again a trend towards miniature varieties, and a renewed interest in the species.

All of us who grow Pansies and Violas should be on the alert for beautiful or unusual natural variations. It would be tedious, and almost certainly impossible, to list all the hybrid Pansies, and species and hybrid Violas in cultivation, other than to remind readers of the winter flowering Pansies.

Due to the efforts and ingenuity of the plant breeders over the last one hundred years, the flowering season of the garden Pansy is very different to what it was in the 1890's. Despite Robert Furber's optimistic assessment of 1730: 'Pansy or Heart's-ease are all quick growers, and so hardy that I hardly have known a Month pass without seeing one or other of them in Flower, even in the hardest Frost', in Victorian England, when the flush of spring bloom was at an end they were deemed to be 'comparatively useless' for summer and autumn display.

Today, cultivars such as *Floral Dance* and *Universal* have been especially selected to tolerate low temperatures and poor light. Sutton's *Azure Blue*, although not traditionally a winter flowering cultivar, is said to put up a spirited performance.

Several of the smaller nurseries can supply the species and cultivars most worthy of garden cultivation. All the large seed companies offer a baffling choice. The Cambridgeshire firm of J.W. Boyce specialise in Pansies. One of their customers reported that their Soham Surprise Mixture was so good that even the cat admired them.

Cultivation of Pansies and Violas

'I know of no plant so easy to cultivate, and at the same time so difficult to keep from year to year, as the Pansy... It is scarcely possible to point to another tribe of plants so peculiarly the amateur's as this, or one that puzzles him to cultivate more.' The *Gardener's Chronicle* (1849).

The garden Pansy belongs to a genus tolerant of a wide range of soil types and climatic conditions, many cultivars inheriting a wilful determination to flower for almost 12 months of the year.

Pansies and Violas require similar conditions below ground, a deep, rich, moisture retentive but free draining humus, incorporating leaf mould, well rotted manure and sharp sand, and firm planting in a firm soil. Above ground, both need protection from cutting winds, but whilst the Pansy delights in sunshine, tolerating little more than a nuance of shadow before hastening towards a gangling decline, the Viola cringes at the edge of baking borders, luxuriating in moist partial shade.

In the nineteenth century, Pansies and Violas were grown with great skill and dedication in the industrial areas of the north, leaf mould, grit and dried cow manure being brought home in baskets and bandannas from country walks.

In the south, autumn planting should be attempted. A hundred years ago there were complaints that nurseries persisted in supplying stock only in the spring, and the same frustration can be met with today.

Despatching plants in 1888.

'To the Ladies and Gentlemen who take pleasure in the flower garden... that as much as the poor, sickly, half-starved, ragged, disconsolate man differs from the same man when prosperous, well-fed, well-clothed, in health, cheerful, and at his ease, so much does the healthy, well-cultivated flower differ from the same flower when neglected, and planted in barren and improper soil.' Thomas Hogg, Florist (1839).

* Some weeks, or even months, before the Pansies and Violas are due to arrive from the Nursery or are ready to be released from their seedling homes, deeply dig the chosen areas of ground. Incorporate into the top nine inches a generous quantity of well rotted cow manure, or home-made compost, leaf mould when available, and a dusting of bonemeal, seaweed meal and weathered soot.

* Before planting, firm by either treading or rolling. Pansies particularly dislike a spongy soil. Sacrifice immediate results in favour of long-term prosperity by removing all buds and flowers. To eradicate any pests lurking amongst the foliage, dip in a solution of 2oz. of soft soap to 1 gallon of water.

* Having prepared a suitable site, take the trouble to excavate a comfortable home. There is neither sense nor profit in scooping out a planting hole indistinguishable from the dustbowl of a basking sparrow. As a final gesture, plant accompanied by a bucket of equal parts of loam, leaf mould and horticultural sand, sifting it around the roots and settling the plant in with the collar level with the surface of the soil.

* Treat plants received through the post to a brief spell of convalescence. Dibble into a bucket of moist compost, syringe the foliage, and place in a shady corner near the back door where they will not be forgotten.Sprinkle regularly with luke warm water, and in a couple of days they will be sufficiently refreshed to take their place in the garden.

* Watering in hot or dry weather, preferably in the evening, will greatly enhance the quality and longevity of the blooms. Mulching is, of course, as beneficial to Violas and Pansies as to all other cultivated areas of the garden.

* James Simkins, a 19th century authority on the Pansy, was convinced that an application of weathered soot in the spring improved the colours and intensified the markings. Follow with a mulch of grass mowings to prevent splashing of the foliage.

> *'It must have systematic treatment, or it never justifies its occupation of the soil.'* Shirley Hibberd *The Amateur's Flower Garden* (1892).

* Since it is unreasonable to expect months of blossom on a starvation diet, a foliar feed at intervals throughout the summer, and a dressing of well rotted manure or other organic supplement after cutting back in the autumn, will be amply repaid.

* The removal of spent flowers is of primary importance.It is not impossible to filter in to the daily routine a few minutes pottering amongst the Pansies, neatly utilising those otherwise barren moments spent waiting for the coffee to percolate, the sauce to prove or the pub to open. Some specialists advise the removal of all flowers at intervals throughout the summer to give these tireless little plants the opportunity for a brief siesta.

* Any tendency to legginess can be countered by cutting back to one joint above ground level, feeding, and earthing up. Established plants should be cut back in late autumn. Premature deterioration can be due to ignorance of this simple task.

This catalogue of duties may read like a lifetime's commitment to one species, but the number of Pansies likely to be grown in a private garden will inflict on their keepers only the lightest, most spasmodic obligations.

Growing Pansies for exhibition is a specialist activity. There are a number of publications, listed in the bibliography, that cover all aspects of this absorbing and controversial hobby.

Propagation

'If any are so curious as to have of these flow'ry decorations in their Gardens, [they] must take Care to provide themselves of Seed or young Plants of ye best kinds.' Peter Aram (1720s).

The garden Pansy differs culturally from the hardier and more perennial Viola in that an almost continual display for nine or more months of the year from these large flowered hybrids can only be sustained by frequent, preferably annual, renewal of the stock.

Seed

* Ideally, seed should be sown from mid to late summer, for transplanting to permanent positions in the autumn. Seeds of winter flowering Pansies must be sown by July, for transplanting in September. An early spring sowing, in gentle heat, will procure flowering plants the same season, but some may think this practice makes extravagant demands on a willing plant.

* If collecting ones own seed, save it from the fresh young blooms of May and June in preference to the rather weary flowers of August and September. No plant should be asked to develop more than two seed pods at a time. To be certain of capturing the seeds before they are ejected around the garden, test for ripeness (brown seeds) by gently squeezing the end of the capsule; the husk will open out sufficiently to gauge the development of the contents. Maturity is also indicated by a straightening of the stem at its junction with the seed pod. If you are likely to be absent over the critical period, enclose in a tiny gauze bag.

* Fill deep seed boxes or pots to 1in. of the top with the chosen compost. Most of us have, perhaps gratefully, dispensed with the 'great mystery and magic ritual' of mixing our own. A seed bed of moist Vermiculite is said to lessen the chance of seedlings damping off. Immerse pots in water until soaked through.

* Press seeds gently into the surface of the soil but do not cover. Some experts recommend covering the trays with paper. In bygone days,

gardeners used glass, shaded by a cabbage leaf. (A hat lined with a cabbage leaf is proof against the hottest day). However, since any covering can all too easily be forgotten, fatally retarding the emerging seedlings, rather select a shady site, protect with netting from the attentions of birds and your own and other people's cats, and keep moist. If seed pots are enclosed in a plastic bag, spray with liquid copper fungicide against damping off.

Fortunately fresh Pansy seed is so precocious that it will usually survive the most inhospitable conditions, although these are not, of course, to be recommended.

The Young Gardiner's Director of 1716 recommended that hard or old seed be 'soaked in a mixture of milk and cow dung', surely an effective restorative for all but the most moribund seeds. The astute gardener made sure that poor quality seed never came into his possession. 'Skillful Gardiners make triall of the Seeds, before they buy them, whether they be good or no, by Putting them into Water gently Boyled; And if they bee good, they will sprout within halfe an Houre.' [10]

Unless subjected to extremes of heat or cold, seeds should germinate within three weeks. Optimum temperatures are 50°F(10°C) - 70°F(21°C). Prick out when large enough to handle; time and labour can be saved by sowing into soil blocks for direct transfer to their final situation, although the deeply rooting Pansy should not be abandoned in such cramped conditions for too long.

> *'That pleasurable species of interest which the production of a novelty produces in the human mind, is perhaps more frequently felt, enjoyed, and witnessed within the pale of the flower garden, than on any other spot of the earth's surface.'* The Florists Museum (1837).

Possibly to the chagrin of ambitious hybridists, many memorable new cultivars of Pansies and Violets have come about independently of man's intervention. If an isolated corner of the garden can be spared, segregate a few Pansies or Violas, and rely on nature to take her course. At best it can be an amusing, even exciting, diversion; at worst, a few ill-favoured seedlings best consigned to the compost heap.Hand pollination is a delicate and laborious business. A brief summary of the technique is given by William Cuthbertson in *Pansies, Violas and Violets.* It is surely unreasonable that such a fecund species is all too often retailed as a forlorn single specimen, at a cost comparable to a whole packet of healthy seeds capable of enamelling a large flower bed with their iridescent blooms.

Cuttings

Although specific colours can be obtained as seed from the major seed merchants and some specialist nurseries, most of us have favourite Pansies, possibly self-sown hybrids, that we would like to perpetuate for ourselves, or for which we receive requests from friends.

It has been said that if healthy, robust children, or healthy robust chickens are desired, it is well to be careful about the parentage, so resolve never to propagate from any plant with a puny constitution. Many professional gardeners maintain that cuttings from strong plants produce better quality stock than either seed or divisions and do, of course, perpetuate the habit peculiar to each variety.

* Spring: Old plants which have been cropped back in the autumn will be offering up a multitude of crisp young shoots suitable for cuttings.

* July: Open out the foliage of mature plants to encourage fresh young growth from the centre. Reserve the energy in these few chosen plants by disbudding for the remainder of the summer. Take cuttings in September.

* Prepare a pot or box about 4ins. in depth. A proprietary compost bulked up with horticultural sand, peat and perlite is a common choice. If Pansies could express an opinion, sand and leaf mould would almost certainly be preferred.

* Select sturdy stems, the joints not more than ½ - 1in. apart; hollow stems will not root.

* Cut cleanly through the stem, just below a joint, to secure a cutting 2½ - 3ins. in length. Trim off the leaves from the lower portion. Make holes with a flat sided dibber; sprinkle in a little sand (an unrivalled rooting medium); insert the cutting up to half its length. It should be firm enough not to pull out.

* Water well before placing in a shaded frame, or a shady and sheltered part of the garden. In my experience, Pansy cuttings do not take kindly to being incarcerated in a plastic bag, rooting quite obligingly in the open air.

Pansies are hardy plants. The frame is to protect them from predators, not from bracing breezes.

Spring cuttings will be ready for transplanting in the autumn. It would be kinder to over-winter autumn cuttings in a sunny, but unheated frame. They will be invaluable for filling in those perplexing and irritating gaps that so often appear at the front of borders in the spring.

Now that handlights are once again available, although it is to be regretted that elegant glass bell jars have been replaced by functional plastic, small numbers of cuttings can be struck under cover. Gardeners soon discover that soft, receptive cuttings root more swiftly when in contact with the abrasive surface of a clay flower pot. An alternative method out of doors is to bury tiles 3ins. deep and 3ins. apart in a suitable cutting mixture, 6ins. in depth. Insert the cuttings firmly along the rows of tiles and keep well watered. If it were convenient to position the cutting bed on the lee side of fruit bushes, these would serve the dual purpose of filtering chilling winds and converting parching sunlight into dappled shade.Cuttings raised out of doors tend to be more robust, although less cosmetically attractive.

Division (Violas only)

Where only a small number of additional plants is required, division is a satisfactory remedy. In late summer, two to three weeks before dividing, cut down to encourage fresh sturdy growth. On lifting, tease out each clump into separate parts. Alternatively, take advantage of new growth in the spring, although there is a risk that the task will be left too late, condemning the separated young plants to hostile conditions before they are sufficiently established to withstand them. Resolutions made at the time to cosset juvenile or vulnerable plants are rarely fulfilled. Before re-planting Violas, trim back the old tough roots. Even experienced gardeners can be timorous about interfering with a plant's nether regions but, on occasion, root pruning has much the same beneficial effect below ground as barbering the foliage has above it.

Congested clumps of Violas should be taken pity on in the autumn, the divided plants settled in to more spacious accommodation.

Layers (Pansies)

Peg down long growths with a hairpin or length of wire, covering the horizontal stems with leafmould. Sever after rooting has taken place.

Violas in Pots

'Tuffts or Bunches of them will look very prittily in Pots...' Peter Aram (1720s).

Both species and hybrid Violas make charming pot plants for an unheated north or north-east facing greenhouse or conservatory. Although they will not flourish under permanent imprisonment indoors, it is a simple matter to allocate a few to the house when making divisions in the autumn.

* Pot up in a rich, open, well drained compost.

* Place pots in a south-facing frame embedded in straw, leaves or weathered ashes to prevent them freezing through. Only close down if the weather is exceptionally severe.

* Pinch out all flower buds until the plants have become established.

* When bringing in in January, drop into a larger outer pot, packing the intervening space with moss or sand to maintain an even temperature to the roots. Stand in saucers filled with silver sand and shredded charcoal.

A practical Victorian device, a clay pot with matching liner.

Violas in pots can look particularly delightful in Victorian flower stands. Irresistible in the shop or auction room, back at home these wire frames can be surprisingly difficult to furnish with flowers.

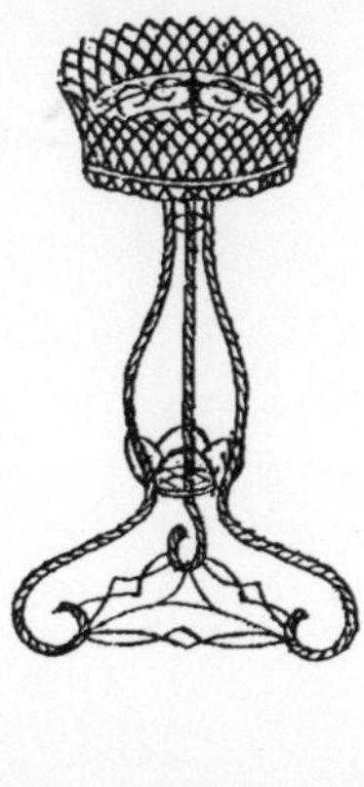

Design in the garden

'A Flower-Garden is now become a necessary appendage of every fashionable residence, and hence it is more frequently left to the discretion of the Gardener, than arranged by the guidance of genuine taste in the owner.' Maria Jackson *The Florists Manual* (1827).

For most of us these days, the only gardener on the premises is ourselves, so few of us have the opportunity to delegate either digging or design to some hired factotum. Yet, in the garden, beautiful and sympathetic arrangements of Pansies and Violas remain an exception. The comeliness of the flowers is of such a flamboyant and diverse kind, that to associate them with contrasting species other than small spring bulbs, which will have sunk to rest before the Pansies and Violas reach their prime, seems to diminish, rather than enhance both parties to the arrangement, although the Pansy would probably be judged the victor in the contest.

Pansies are too often recommended as appropriate ground cover beneath roses, a scheme that is neither practical nor artistically commendable. It is no easy task to delve out a home for the deeply rooting Pansy between the tough, but vulnerable roots of the roses. Additionally, dead heading of both groups then becomes impossible. Far better to employ the hardy geraniums, which seem impervious to any amount of cultural abuse.

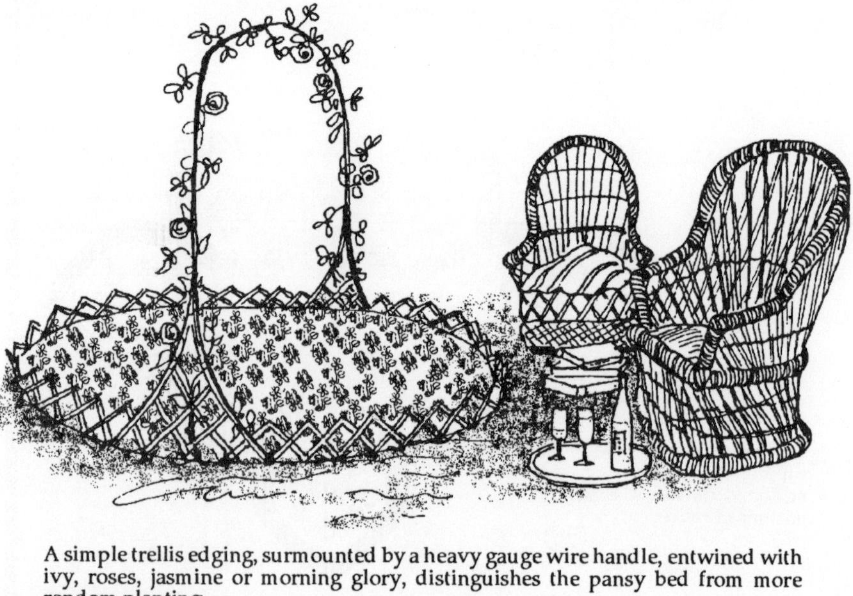

A simple trellis edging, surmounted by a heavy gauge wire handle, entwined with ivy, roses, jasmine or morning glory, distinguishes the pansy bed from more random planting.

The acerbic William Robinson, theoretically a ferocious opponent of bedding out, was nonetheless convinced that 'Pansies in great variety' were worthy of special treatment and should be displayed 'away from the confusion and weariness of the ordinary flower border.'

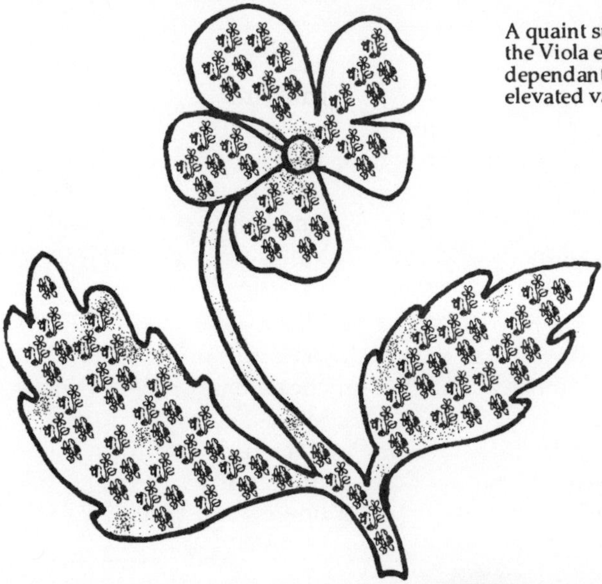

A quaint suggestion for the Viola enthusiast, but dependant for effect on an elevated vantage point.

A simple Knot garden outlined in box hedging, suited to Pansies, Violas, and small bulbs.

Once established, an almost labour free small garden, pretty and practical throughout the year.

1. Outer area of paving, gravel or grass.
2. Box (Buxus sempervirens) clipped at two feet.
3. Pansies and dwarf bulbs (Snowdrops, Scilla siberica, Iris reticulata, Muscari tubergenianum (ice blue), Cyclamen coum).
4. Dwarf box (Buxus sempervirens suffruticosa).
5. Topiary, in box.

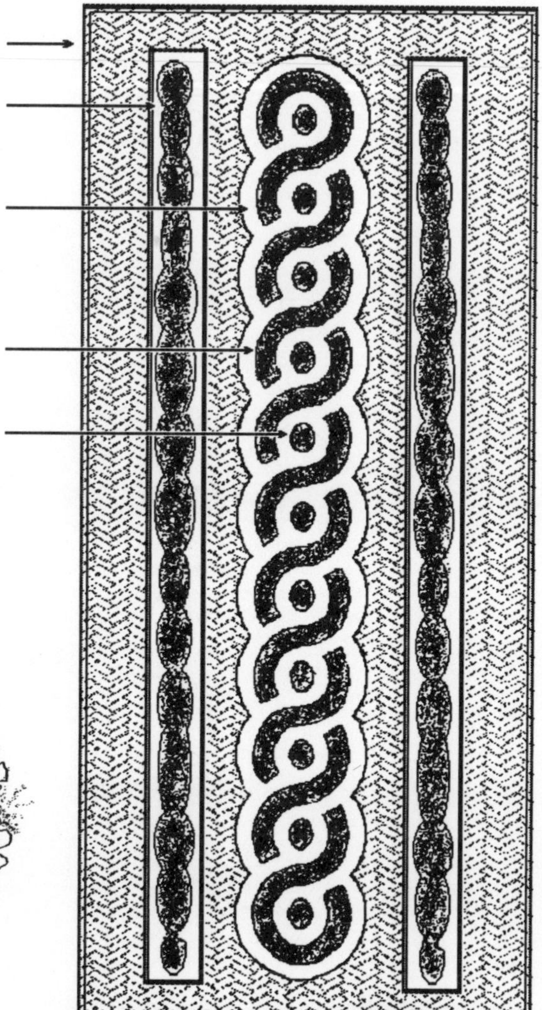

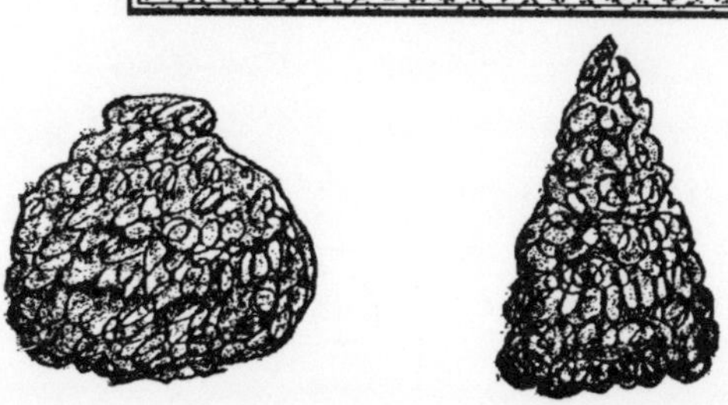

Since winter-flowering Pansies always confound the sceptics, surely more of us should make the effort to have at least one large tub or window box of these courageous little flowers in some sheltered, sunny corner to illuminate grey winter days.

Hanging flower pot.

A lined wicker basket packed with moss for Pansies or Violets in a cool conservatory. The wreath of ivy will remain fresh for many weeks.

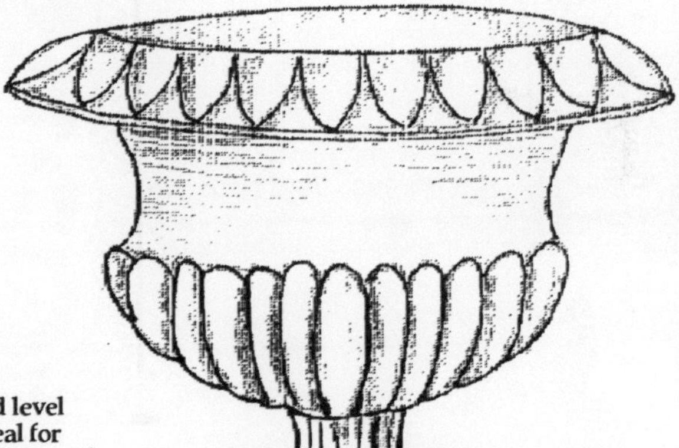

Stone urns at ground level are, aesthetically, ideal for Pansies, but must be watered daily in dry weather.

'*Our little favourite early gained for itself a distinguished place in the trim borders of our ancestor's gardens.*' Shirley Hibberd (1857).

A seventeenth century design for a Knot garden.

Pansies and Violas associate happily with the smaller spring bulbs, forget-me-nots, bellis daisies, and other species that offer companionship rather than competition. But they can be at their most seductive in some isolation, shamelessly cherished for their pretty ways.

Decorative and useful. Dwarf topiary gives year round interest to a bed edged with chives and thyme. The edible Pansy is a valid companion to parsley, marjoram, basil, savory, and other neat and docile herbs. If situated near the kitchen door, rippling cobblestones ensure dry all-weather access.

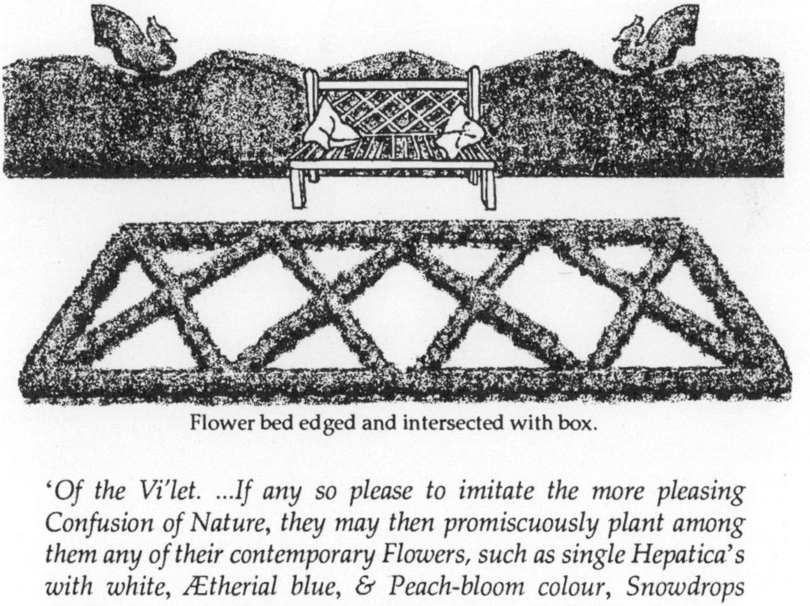

Flower bed edged and intersected with box.

'Of the Vi'let. ...If any so please to imitate the more pleasing Confusion of Nature, they may then promiscuously plant among them any of their contemporary Flowers, such as single Hepatica's with white, Ætherial blue, & Peach-bloom colour, Snowdrops double & single, Primroses several colours, Daffodils, Crocus's, Grape Flow'rs & such like suitable things.' [11]

Spring Flowers.

Sweet Violets

Viola Odorata, © RBG Kew.

'If there is one flower more than another that can lay claim to the honour of being everybody's favourite, it is the Violet; it cheers the most saddened spirits, and gladdens the most robust.' H. Cannell's *Illustrated Floral Guide* (1883).

Herb, emblem, symbol, fragrance, unguent, comfit, the last scented perennial of autumn and the earliest and most secretive of spring's blossoms. In folklore and literature, the Violet remains the best loved of our wild flowers. More than three hundred years ago, John Parkinson wrote of his 'choise flower of delight': 'The Garden Violets are so well knowne unto all, that either keepe a Garden, or hath but once come into it, that I shall but lose labour and time to describe that which is so common.'

At one time tossed in to drinks, strewn on floors, serenaded in verse, distilled into perfumes, paraded in buttonholes, clasped to bosoms, masticated as salads, and festooned on hats. Yet today it is probably one of the least cultivated of our native garden plants.

'The flower of the Violet', says Professor Henslow, 'is very curious in several respects. In the first place, it is upside down, as the stalk is twisted...The way in which the leaves have their edges rolled up, before they are expanded, is peculiar... The flower is irregular, the petals and other parts not all of the same shape.' [12]

To compound its oddities, the Violet is cleisto-gamous or self-fertilising from closed flowers, the term deriving from two Greek words meaning 'enclosed' and 'union'. But in one respect, Professor Henslow under-estimates his subject. 'The Violet family', he claims, 'does not contain any plants of much use to man.' However, herbals both ancient and modern reveal that the Violet is almost a pharmacy in itself, leaf and flower yielding infusions that soothe afflictions as disparate as a mild headache and cancer of the throat.

Although we tend to associate Violets with the secret enchantments of sheltered English lanes, they are members of a family widely distributed over the greater part of the globe. In size and beauty the flower of the Violet is eclipsed by many thousand other inhabitants of the floral kingdom; perhaps it is the tantalisingly fleeting nature of the delicious scent that holds us in thrall to this demure gem, a response rather prosaically induced by the substance ionine temporarily dulling our olfactory senses.

Francis Bacon, the seventeenth century philosopher, statesman, essayist and gardener, declared: 'The daintiest Smells of Flowers, are out of those Plants, whose leaves smell not: as Violets'. A surprising assertion from one whose practical interest in science was such that he died, in 1626, from a chill caught whilst stuffing a fowl with snow, intending to observe the affect of cold on the preservation of flesh. Yet disturb the leaves of a clump of sweet Violets stripped of flowers, and the scent released will be as powerful as that to be enjoyed from a nosegay of blooms.

The hardy *Viola odorata* is indigenous to the British Isles. The origins of the tender Parma Violet remain obscure, although generally believed to be of oriental origin.

The more usually single, occasionally double, *Viola odorata* satisfied the needs, and satiated the senses of our ancestors for hundreds of years. But by the beginning of the 18th century, advances in scientific and horticultural knowledge incited the ambitious nurseryman and private gardener to improve on what nature had given them.

'I must have a large bunch of white Parma Violets'. Lady Ida Sitwell.

Parma Violet *Comte de Brazza (Swanley White).*

Certainly Parmas were known in this country in 1816, the gardener to Sir Joseph Banks, President of the Royal Society, plant collector and unofficial Director of Kew Gardens under George III, cultivating three hundred of these Violets in pots at Sir Joseph's garden at Isleworth.

In France they had been known simultaneously as *La Violette de Parme* and *La Violette de Naples*. English growers, after dithering between the names Neopolitan and Parma, eventually opted for the latter.

A blandishment to an employer, or commemoration of a personality fleetingly in favour, has burdened many a lovely bloom with a discordant name. More fortunate, two Parma Violets, *Marie Louise* and *Duchesse de Parme* are associated melodiously with Napoleon's second wife. With *Comte de Brazza (Swanley White)* they are the only Parmas still generally available.

These three exotic Violets can still conjure up echoes of an era of elegance and luxury. Of perfumed flowers pinned to muffs as pretty girls skimmed over frozen lakes, of carriages crowding through snow-packed streets towards glittering evenings at the opera, of scented ballrooms, Strauss waltzes, flirtation and requited love.

It has been suggested that Sir Joseph Banks's gardener, Isaac Oldacre, may also have been responsible for the introduction of the hardy Russian Violets, since he had previously been chief gardener to the Czar. [13] If that is so, it was some thirty years before their impact on the development of the cultivated Violet became apparent.

Mr. Shackell of the Lockbrook Nursery near Bristol was one of the first to benefit professionally from this foreign hardy strain, with their sweetly scented flowers. Of necessity combining kitchen gardening with his aspirations as a Florist - 'I can seldom allow Violets to have the undivided occupation of any piece of ground' - he observed that they were noticeably more vigorous when co-habiting with onions. Whether or not this was a contributory factor, in 1848 he created a sensation 'with the aid of tireless advertising by the raiser', with his new cultivar *Russian Superb.*

Fifteen years later F.J. Graham of Cranford in Middlesex bred *The Czar*, not far from the garden where these Russian Violets may have established their first English home. In 1865 *The Czar* was the first Violet to receive the Royal Horticultural Society's First Class Certificate, the Society recognising his astonishing seedling as 'undoubtedly one of the finest hardy Violets in cultivation.'

Another market gardener, initially engaging in Violets for the cut flower trade as a sideline, was George Lee of Clevedon in Somerset. Declaring that 'the old Russian is one that has not its equal in every particular', he crossed *The Czar* with *Devoniensis* to create, in 1873, the greatly admired deep blue Violet *Victoria Regina* with blooms more than an inch across.

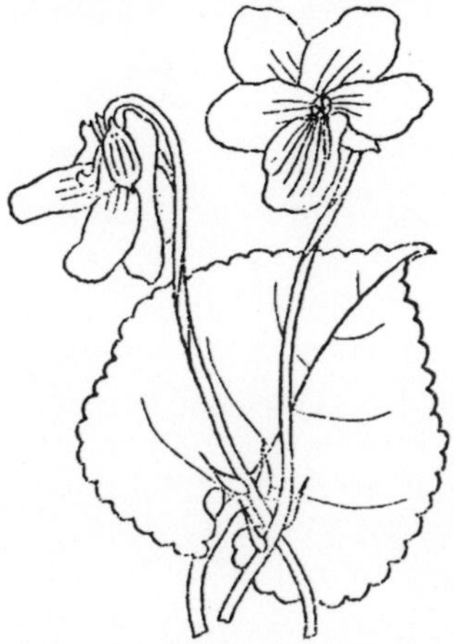

This simple sketch of George Lee's *Victoria Regina* accompanied his advice on Violet culture offered to the readers of the *Florist and Pomologist* in December, 1873.

Soon George Lee's Violets were an asset to both the family and the town, as recorded in the *Clevedon Mercury* of 1883: 'Many hundreds of thousands of bunches have gone by rail and post this season to all parts of the world, for the Clevedon Violets, thanks to our old and esteemed friend, George Lee, are now a household word. We have been assured on the most reliable authority that our postal bags have been redolent with the perfume of this once lowly, now Queenly, flower and that the perfume crept out of our Railway Parcel Office to the astonishment of strangers.'

Recently Violet plants have been removed from the abandoned site of Lee's nursery, and are being propagated under the auspices of The National Council for the Conservation of Plants and Gardens, so perhaps before too long we shall once again be able to indulge our senses with the heady perfume of George Lee's Violets, and make fragrant the postman's sack as we consign small parcels to discerning friends.

Welcomed in France, the progeny inheriting the genes from these hardy Russian Violets were adopted by the 'patient genius', Armand Millet to breed a race of large flowered hybrids, such as the lovely single cultivar *Princesse de Galles* (Princess of Wales), which remains the most popular of the hardy cut flower varieties. Although Englishmen such as Shackell, Graham and Lee combined dedication, perseverance and luck to transform insignificant wild species into exotic florist's flowers, it was the work of Frenchmen such as Armand Millet which established the Violet as a major commercial crop.

Before long, imports of French Violets, grown in a more benign climate, were flooding the English market. In 1874 'Fair readers' of *Domestic Floriculture* were advised that the perfumed flowers to be found in the pretty flacons on their dressing tables almost certainly originated from 'the paradise of Violets', the south of France, some 13,000 lbs. of Violet blossoms being harvested each year. The insatiable appetite of the cut flower trade ensured that the gentle Violet contributed notably to the fortunes of many commercial growers in both France and England, 'ladies particularly finding the industry a profitable and pleasing one to engage in.'

The patronage of Queen Victoria and Princess Alexandra transformed the Violet into a flower of fashion. Three thousand plants annually were grown under frames at Windsor to satisfy the requirements of the royal family and the court. The royal fancy percolated down the social scale; in the 1890's *The Gardener*'s *Chronicle* reported that 'thousands of city clerks appear at the office every morning with a fresh bunch of Violets in their buttonholes.' With the approach of autumn, flowergirls, with baskets piled high with Violets, were a familiar sight in most cities, the polluted air 'laden with their fragrance.'

Country Life were assured of a market for their publication *Sweet Violets and Pansies*, since 'in almost every garden an attempt is made to grow a few clumps in a frame.'

But by the 1880's fog, frost and snow were devastating the English harvest and the livlihood of women pickers was at risk as the growers' incomes plummeted from the £50 or £60 a week secured in previous seasons.

Yet for the man or woman departing the shores of England to do, and possibly to die, in some torrid foreign land, the gentle Violet retained its powers, a last lingering symbol of dew-drenched hedgerows and soft spring skies. 'When you can no longer buy them in the streets or in the less expensive shops, there is one place where you may get them on a Friday morning. It is at a great railway station at which people who are going forth to serve the Empire begin their long journey. Here they sell so readily that the price is apt to be exorbitant - if it were possible to consider the charges of a merchant who gave you Violets in exchange for a mere matter of money.' [14]

The opportunity to treat a friend, a lover, or oneself to a nosegay of Violets was not extinguished until more recent times. In the 1930's Grace Zambra, herself a nurserywoman and an authority on the genus, reported that acres in Kent, Sussex and Devonshire were still devoted to their culture, some fifty nurseries specialising in this paragon amongst florist's flowers. A diminished acreage continued to be tended into the 1960's, but today most florists assailed by a request for Violets automatically assume that it is the erroneously labelled African Violet that one has in mind. Consequently, many of the cultivars that enticed customers a century ago are not only unobtainable in the trade but quite possibly extinct.

Whilst one can understand that a crop demanding skilled attention is no longer commercially viable for other than the dedicated specialist nursery, it is surely very perverse of today's private gardeners to have so universally abandoned a hardy, in the case of Parmas slightly tender, beautiful, fragrant, winter-flowering species.

These losses reflect badly on our present capacity to appreciate the more subtle joys of life, seemingly placated for many months of the year by the ubiquitous pot chrysanthemum, and satisfied by the leathery evergreens of few demands and fewer compensations.

This is by no means a new complaint. As long ago as 1905, contributors to horticultural journals were pleading for classes for Violets at winter shows. 'Probably in some instances they are left unheeded simply and for no other reason than that they are forgotten by schedule committees when labouring under such unbounded zeal for the chrysanthemum'. [15]

If Sweet Violets again become commercially available, the convalescent's bedside table could be relieved of the clutter of huge, barren blooms, and a whole ward enveloped in the sharp, rich, fugitive fragrance of a small vase of Violets. Quite a modest bunch would refresh the sterile atmosphere of the air conditioned office complex.

'There is scarcely a garden so small that it will not furnish a few bright flowers.' T.C.March *Flower & Fruit Decoration* (1862).

Those of us with larger gardens are constantly being lectured on the limitations of the tiny plots doled out to even the more costly of today's new homes. Armand Millet maintained that the cultivation of Violets in small gardens was a frugal hobby within the competence of all.

Violet Odoratissima.

Even today, plants are cheap to purchase, or free from friends. The Misses A. and D. Allen-Brown, who grew Violets commercially at Henfield in Sussex in the twenties and thirties, started with ' a very small but sunny garden, a couple or so of frames, some elderly tools and much cheerful self-confidence.'

Has the spirit of enterprise and adventure utterly deserted the gard eners of the 1980s?

Cultivation of Violets

'Violets must have sympathy, a good atmosphere, an open position and well drained soil... we may add to the botanical description the following characteristics; firm, but obliging; scent variable, responsive to kindness; discriminating in living longer for some people than for others; quiet, but never depressing; whimsical, very.' The Misses A. & D. Allen-Brown.

It is reasonable to assume that the cultivated Violet requires conditions akin to the native wild flower. Confronted with the option of making do or dying, Violets will persist, if not actually prosper, in the most impoverished and depressing situations, but these will not be the plants from which we gather the large, long stemmed, fragrant flowers that dispel the gloom of a dull November and suspend a rainbow of optimism over a freezing February. Nor do they respond to being treated as pampered darlings. Of an independent mien, fresh, clean air, good food, ample refreshment, summer shade and winter sun are the sum total of their demands.

Disturbed as many of us are about the pollutants contaminating our air and water, one advantage today's city gardener has over his Victorian counterpart is that the air is, in many respects, much cleaner than it was a hundred years ago. The fine hairs on the underside of the Violet leaf trap dirt and block the breathing pores; the sulphurous, fog-laden atmosphere that at one time blanketed city streets ensured that Violets promptly perished if cultivated within twelve miles of any large British town.

Situation

Under the hedge all safe and warm
Sheltered from boisterous wind and storm,
We Violets lie;
With each small eye,
Closely shut whilst the cold goes by.

The Language of Flowers and the Poetry of Flowers.

In these times of busy schedules and little, if any, paid help in the garden, the siting of the Violet bed is, of necessity, something of a compromise. In bygone days when time and effort were of little moment, Violets spent the summer months in north or east-facing sheltered borders, awaiting transfer to south-facing frames or beds for the duration of the winter. Where this arrangement is now impracticable, a south-facing site, sheltered from northerly and easterly winds, must be chosen, since maximum winter sunshine has priority over summer shade.

As compensation, decorative or edible crops such as peas (culinary and sweet), ornamental gourds, tall herbs such as Dill or Fennel, the larger salad varieties or even fruit bushes can be employed to ensure dappled shade throughout the summer. In these unnatural conditions, exceptional care must be taken to keep the ground of the Violet bed cool and moist. Violets find the rich soil of a vegetable plot much to their taste, and as the Violet bed should be moved every third or fourth year, this preference fits neatly into the rotation pattern of even a small kitchen garden.

Many nineteenth century nurserymen combined Violet culture with general market gardening, and discovered that it made sound horticultural sense to locate the Violet beds beneath the dappled shade of the orchard.

'And beds of Violets blooming 'midst the trees,
Load with waste fragrance the nocturnal breeze'.

The Allen-Browns were unusual in recommending full exposure to the sun throughout the year, estimating that the benefits of summer sunshine on the ripening crowns could be parried by constant watering to keep the dreaded Red Spider mite at bay, despite the apparently welcoming conditions.

As one expert insists that Violet beds must run from east to west, so another proclaims that all will be lost unless they incline from north to south. The only opinion in common is that it is impossible for the Violet to entertain too much winter sunshine.

Soil

'*And the earth well laboured and turned in with dung.*' Thomas Hyll (1563).

An exemplary compost for Violets would be one that combined the seemingly conflicting qualities of being both retentive and free draining. George Lee knew that the soil should be porous as well as rich: 'Some of our best wild Violets grow in hedgerows, and hedgerows are generally a little elevated... which implies good drainage.'

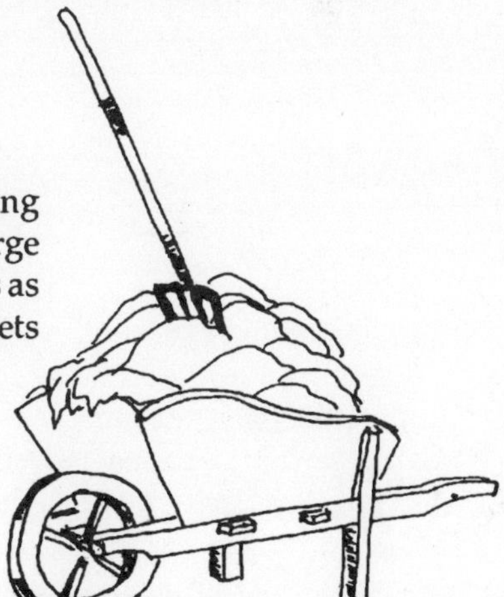

In cultivating sweet Violets, we are merely magnifying natural conditions to boost the vigour of the plant and the quality and quantity of the flowers. Consequently the ideal compost will be that which imitates most closely the soil in which the wild Violet flourishes - a mix of loam and leaf mould, with the addition of decayed manure and liquid feeds to compensate for the artificial performance we are exacting from a simple hedgerow flower. Leaves which have rotted where they fell are superior to stacked, fermented leaves. Excessive feeding will encourage foliage at the expense of flowers. Violets do not choose a chalky soil, and dislike an acid one. A pH of 6.0 to 6.5 is ideal.

* Having selected the site, dig over deeply during the winter months. The roots of the tiny Violet extend at least one foot through the soil, and a depth of three feet is not unknown.

* Incorporate as much compost and leaf mould as come to hand - oak leaves for preference. (Mould means mould, not raw leaves). Add 1oz. of Sulphate of Potash and the same of Bonemeal to the square yard. A determined attempt should be made to procure seaweed meal, stocked by organic mail order companies. The minerals in seaweed have a remarkable effect on the health and vigour of all plants. Distribute at 4oz. to the square yard when preparing the bed.

* Leave fallow for a few weeks for frost to condition the earth and birds to glean pests ejected from their winter quarters. In the early spring, tread or roll to compress the soil. Firm conditions are essential for happy Violets. However, beds should be sufficiently narrow for future cultivation to be carried out without trampling on the ground; there is a difference between compression and compaction.

* Finally, before planting, work in a light dressing of weathered soot. (Weathered means leaving in an open bin, in an open but dry shed, for at least three months, not discarding in a leaching heap in a corner of the garden). The local Sweep will almost certainly oblige. Too often nowadays nutritious ingredients, available on the premises, or free on request, are neglected in favour of some expensive, but widely advertised, commercial concoction.

Planting

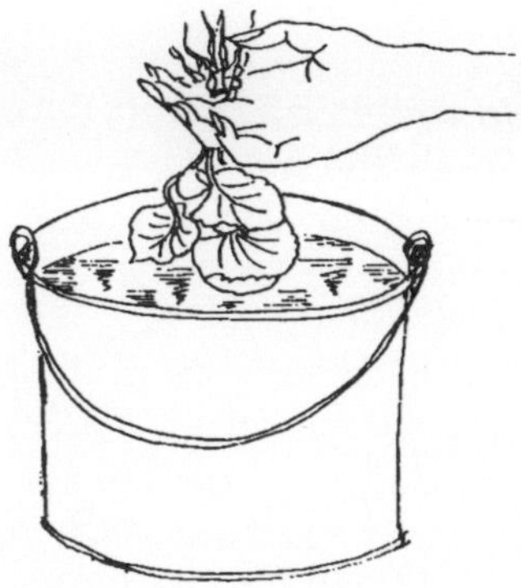

- * Before planting out, briefly immerse bought-in stock, and your own propagated material, in a solution of 2oz. soft soap to 1 gallon of water.

- * Space generously, at least 1ft.-18ins. apart. If a mature Violet does not measure one foot across there is something amiss with your technique.

- * Excavate deeply. The hole should oblige the roots, not the roots the hole.

- * Plant firmly, the crown level with the surface of the soil. No leaf should have any part of the stem underground.

- * If transplanting during dry weather is unavoidable, puddle in.

- * Clean off and refresh the foliage by syringing above and beneath the leaves.

- * If hot conditions prevail, cover with a flowerpot during the day, removing and syringing in the evening, until the crop is established.

- * Do not weed for at least a month. Dragging out weeds will do more harm than good. When hoeing can safely be commenced, snick off all runners and harass any grubs that may be lurking just beneath the surface.

- * Once established, mulch regularly, especially in dry weather, with leaf mould, well rotted manure or other suitable material. That tribe of gardeners who annually construct a dilemma from a few boxes of lawn mowings, can put them to beneficial use on the Violet bed.

- * The only additional encouragement required is a liquid feed at two to three week intervals throughout the summer. Plants appreciate a varied diet quite as much as the gardener.

Gertrude Jekyll was satisfied that her own formula for healthy Violets, 'carefully cultivated and liberally enriched', was vindicated when friends exclaimed, 'What a nice batch of young hollyhocks.'

* From the beginning of August encourage and peg down sufficient runners, not more than three to a plant, to take over from the mature plants as next season's crop.

* Parmas destined for over-wintering in cold frames should be transferred in September, hardy Violets in October.

Propagation

Cuttings

It seems to be generally agreed that cuttings taken in September are preferable to those taken in March, although the topic ignited a brisk correspondence in *The Garden* in the 1880's.

* Autumn cuttings, over-wintered in a cold frame or, in the case of hardy single Violets, a south-facing border, are more likely to withstand the rigours of any hot dry summers than the more juvenile stock of early spring. This view was endorsed by Mr. John Dunn, who grew three thousand Violets in frames in the royal gardens at Windsor before the First World War.

* The cutting mix is very much a matter of personal choice. Peat and sand, loam and leaf mould, peat and perlite, sand alone, all have their devotees. Above all, select cuttings from strong, healthy plants. No one ever made a silk purse out of a sow's ear.

* Ensure that each slip has both a crown bud and a few root hairs attached. Remove all lower shoots and runners, leaving the neck clean so that the strength goes into the crown. Above all, once work has commenced, don't dawdle. If interrupted, place the cuttings in water in a shady corner. The objective is short, stiff, and stocky plants.

Violet cutting.

If spring cuttings are preferred, these must **not** be taken from plants after a season under glass, or in pots as the quality of the plant will have been irretrievably impaired.

Runners

* Peg down in August, no more than three runners per plant, after mulching with a tempting rooting medium such as sieved leafmould. Shun runners that start from ground level as these have the reputation of running forever, instead of getting down to the business of incubating next season's crop of flowers. Runners should not be allowed on plants destined for over-wintering in frames.

* Remove all leaves between the crown of the runner and the parent plant.

* Sever in October, not by tugging or cutting, but by passing the fingers beneath the stem at the junction with the parent and exerting gentle downward pressure with the thumb.

Pegged down runner (left) and rooted runner being removed by downward pressure of the thumb.

* If there is sufficient space, rooted runners can be left in the main bed until the spring, or replanted in a reserve bed 4ins. apart. Some comforts, such as a temporary cloche in severe weather, are appreciated.

* Meanwhile, condition their permanent quarters as previously described.

* The exception to runners taken in the autumn are those harvested from framed or cloched Parma Violets in the spring. Runners removed in February or March should be boxed up in suitable compost, and kept in a frame or unheated greenhouse until planting out in their summer quarters in April.

A tenacious propagator from groping runners, neglected hardy Violets can almost become a nuisance, although welcomed as ground cover in conditions where little else will thrive. Yet it is this very generosity in thrusting so many eager offspring out into the world that makes the sweet Violet such a rewarding and thrifty plant to grow.

Division

'Every Body knows that they are propagated by Tufts, that is, by dividing one great Tuft into several little ones, which likewise in time grows thick, and fit to be divided into other little ones.' Jean de La Quintinie (English translation 1693).

* All scented Violets can be increased by division at the completion of the flowering season in the spring. Gently tease the old plants apart. Reserve three crowns and a complement of young feeding roots and root hairs to each division.

* Set out in a shady temporary stock bed 9ins. apart, or 1ft. - 18ins. apart if transferred immediately to their permanent quarters. Ground recently vacated by a heavily manured crop, such as cauliflowers, has been much favoured in the past.

* After the harvesting of divisions, runners and cuttings at the conclusion of the flowering season in the spring, all old plants must be burnt. This is neither as wasteful nor as ruthless as it may sound, as by then there will be a bevy of young plants eager to take their place. The renowned generosity of gardeners should not extend to passing on old, possibly diseased stock to novice gardeners naively grateful for any offering that comes their way.

Seed

'They produce Seed in little reddish Shells or Husks.' Jean de La Quintinie (1693).

Unless required for propagation, seed heads should be removed as they make unnecessary demands on the plant's reserves of energy. As we have mentioned, *Viola odorata* is cleistogamous. The early spring flowers, although cornucopias of honey, usually appear too early for any but the most precocious or foolhardy bee. It is the seemingly immature, self-fertilising, autumn flowers that more usually give birth to the shy but buxom seed capsules. If these mysteriously disappear, it could be because discriminating mice are partial to Violet seeds.

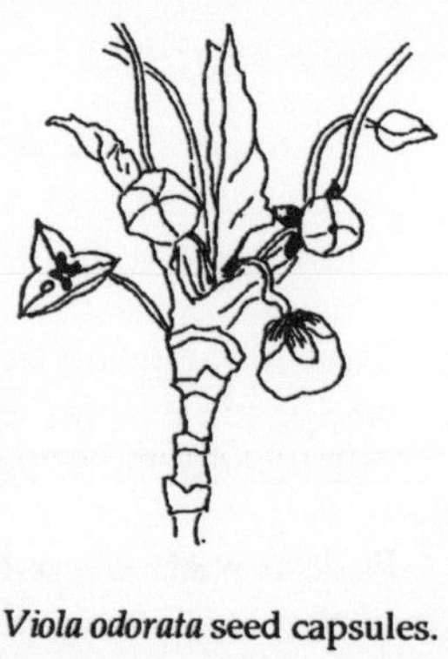

Viola odorata seed capsules.

Sow as soon as ripe, in boxes, in a light friable soil, barely covering the seed. Seed sown in the open ground will almost certainly be forgotten, failure quite probably due to impatient over-planting. The assumption that germination will always be slow and erratic is overly pessimistic; the response of fresh seed can be commendably brisk. Good results are obtained from cold frame or outdoor exposure, providing boxes are kept moist and sheltered. The famed hybridist Armand Millet recommended covering the box with a damp cloth before sinking it in the soil. Some seventeenth century gardeners were satisfied that the only profitable moment to sow Violets was at the full moon in February. Prick out at two pairs of leaves.

A cautionary memorandum; Charles Darwin proved that progeny from cross-fertilised plants were of a sturdier constitution than those grown from self-fertilising, or cleistogamous plants. So other than for an occasional experiment in hybridisation, whether deliberate or accidental, it is more prudent to increase Violets from cuttings, runners or divisions.

Perhaps travellers in foreign lands should not place too much trust in the assumption, rife in the sixteenth century, that 'the seed of Violets will drive away scorpions'.

Violets in frames

'*The Violet nothing behind the best, for Smelling Sweetly.*' William Lawson (1617).

Violets are over-wintered in frames, not so much to protect a hardy, or near-hardy, plant from frost as to protect the blossoms from the tumults and tempests of the winter months; forcing with artificial heat has no role in their cultivation. Most Violets are by nature hardy plants, and not only welcome, but positively insist on, an almost spartan regime of clean, fresh air. Deprived of such moderate demands, Violets in frames will soon decline and perish.

* August: Prepare frames. A southern aspect is essential to capture maximum winter sunlight. If previously tenanted by other crops, such as cucumbers, scrupulously cleanse and disinfect.

* To secure perfect drainage, start with a layer of some loose material; hedge trimmings, or the stalks of last season's michaelmas daisies - indestructible on the compost heap - would do as well. Tread down.

* Follow with at least 1ft. of leaves or old strawy manure or a mixture of the two. A supply of leaves is not dependant on a large country

garden. Some of the leafiest locations in the country are found along suburban roads, and many councils are guilty of annually burning this valuable horticultural resource. Collect up well in advance, incorporate salt, lime and soot, and turn regularly to expel volatile gases.

* Tread down. Add a layer of decayed manure, and firm again.

* Top with 1ft. of soil - equal parts loam and leafmould - supplemented with a sprinkling of bonemeal and weathered soot. Firm again. Some gardeners favour the addition of a small quantity of wood ash and lime rubble.

* The intention is to position the plants with the leaves about 6ins. clear of the glass.

This is a traditional recipe recommended by many professional growers over the last one hundred years. If some of the ingredients are impossible to obtain, experiment with a mixture that is more readily available. The basic essentials are free drainage, plenty of leafmould and firm planting in a firm soil.

Violets in a ventilated frame.

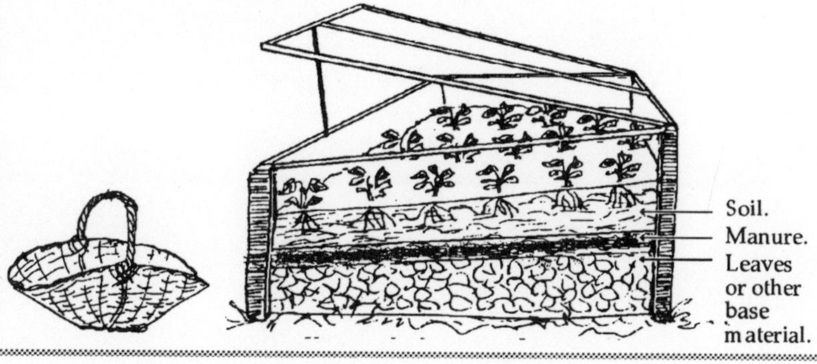

* Transplanting: Parmas in September; Hardy Violets in October, preferably after a touch of frost.

* Select only the very best plants. Strong crowns, the centre of the plant from where the flower buds will emerge, indicate a prolonged and floriferous performance. Plants must be budded up before removal to frames.

* Twenty-four hours before lifting soak thoroughly, and pick off any decaying foliage.

* Peg down and detach any runners destined to remain in the bed.

* Using a fork (a spade could damage fragile roots), take up with as large a root ball as is practicable.

* Settle firmly into the frames, 1ft. apart, the crowns level with the surface of the soil.

* Dust with soot, being careful to avoid the crowns. (Not only is soot a gentle fertiliser, but black soil warms up more quickly.)

* Water with a fine rose to cleanse the foliage.

* A scattering of charcoal will help to absorb excess moisture if the frames have to be closed in cold weather.

* Keep frames aired, but shaded, for a few days: subsequently admit fresh air on every suitable occasion. The temperature should never exceed 60°F(15°C).

* Sashes should be removed altogether on sunny days, although the design of many modern aluminium frames ensures that this is by no means an easy thing to do. However, automatic ventilators do permit the gradual introduction of fresh air as the day warms up. Only in very extreme conditions should frames be closed for any length of time, or covers placed over the glass at night. In these circumstances, the sides of the frames, also, should be protected. Sheets of thick polystyrene, cork tiles or newspaper are all excellent insulators. Straw bales stacked around frames are wonderfully effective, and, if free of pesticides, convert into mulching or composting material in the spring.

* A thorough watering may only be necessary three or four times during the winter season. This should be done in the morning, thus allowing the leaves to dry out before nightfall. Treat to a weak solution of manure water approximately once a fortnight.

* Glass must be kept clear, inside and out, and the interior sweet and clean with the regular removal and disposal of decaying foliage. When washing down, avoid splattering the plants.

Throughout the season contented, but not cosseted, Violets will 'open out genially' and gathering bunches of sweetly perfumed flowers will be one of the more memorable joys of the long winter months. Providing these few simple rules are not overlooked, the management of Violets in frames, William Cuthbertson assures us, 'is done with comparative ease and gratifying success.'

Perhaps a touch of glamour enlivens the daily routine with the knowledge that 'the cultivation of Violets for the purpose of providing plentiful blossoms during winter and the earliest days of spring is an art.'

The longest flowering period will be sustained by removing some plants to a cold frame in the autumn, others to a southern aspect for their winter quarters, leaving the remainder in north or west facing beds. But few of us have either the time or space to carry through such a counsel of perfection.

A compromise would be to cloche a selection of hardy Violets, and all the Parmas, in the situation in which they normally grow, leaving a percentage to confront the winter in the open air. The flowers may not be as large, as prolific nor as perfect as those grown in the more specialised conditions of a carefully prepared frame, but will nonetheless respond sufficiently well for their beauty and fragrance to enrich the dreariest period of the year. If Violets are grown under cover in the open ground, it is advisable to change the site every year.

Anyone tempted to dismiss a crop of Violets as a frivolous luxury should be asked to identify another species that contributes beauty, fragrance and edible foliage, rich in Vitamin C, for six months of the year.

Watering

'Watering in inexperienced hands, is a source of much mischief.'
James Simkins (1889).

Not only is the Violet a thirsty plant, but plain water is superior to any other defence in the enduring conflict between the Red Spider mite and the cultivated Violet. The principal weakness of this pernicious pest is its distaste for moist conditions. In dry summer weather water copiously, directing jets of water beneath the foliage to discomfort any mites contemplating a permanent home. If possible syringe daily, morning and evening. A less intensive regime will be of great benefit to Pansies and Violas.

The advice frequently given, 'little and often', when championing a pleasure or prescribing a tonic should never be applied to watering plants. A thorough soaking at protracted intervals, stopping short of drowning as roots are unable to function in waterlogged conditions, is what is required.

Manure

'For it is usuall to helpe the Ground with Mucke; And likewise to recomfort it sometimes with Mucke put to the Roots.' Francis Bacon (1627).

Black Jack

Suspend a sack containing grass mowings, well rotted manure (scalded with boiling water to kill off pests), and soot in a covered butt of rainwater for several weeks. If necessary, weigh down with a heavy stone. Before use, dilute to the colour of weak tea.

Comfrey

No garden of any size should be without a stock of comfrey. Easy to grow, it can be cultivated in almost any odd corner, between fruit bushes, amongst shrubs or even in a large border. Rich in minerals, particularly calcium and potassium; can be harvested several times in a season. Due to the unrivalled stench of the fermenting leaves, suspension in water is not recommended. For sweeter results, punch holes with a hot poker in the bottom of an old plastic dustbin; position over a discarded washing-up bowl; pack with damp comfrey leaves, pressed down with some heavy object; weigh down the lid to prevent the structure blowing away, and wait for the dark odourless liquid from the decomposing leaves to drip into the bowl. Dilute 10:1.

Seaweed

Readily obtainable in liquid form as a foliar feed.

Even quite small gardens can benefit from investment in a knapsack sprayer. Repeated replenishment of watering cans is both time consuming and tedious and every shrub, flower, fruit and vegetable will prosper under the same nourishing routine as that meted out to the Violets. Another time saving possibility is a liquid dispenser attached to the garden hose.

Varieties

'Downcast dew-drenched eyes,
Summer's breath 'neath winter's skies.'
Joan B. White.

Watercolour and text by Yvonne Mathews.

Nowadays, those of us beguiled by a mirage of winter rooms secreting vases of elusively perfumed, gleaming flowers have to be grateful for the few, the very few, varieties that we can still obtain.

Roy Coombs, in his book *Violets*, lists 278 cultivars that were, at one time, in cultivation. Of the scented cultivars, only thirteen are currently commercially available.

In the opinion of Clive Groves, whose family have been growing Violets since 1866, the following hardy singles are the most suitable for an introductory foray into growing scented Violets.

Coeur d'Alsace: Deep rosy salmon; good perfume. Suitable for rockeries.

The Czar: Deep purple. Scented and long stemmed. Popular with the cut flower market.

Luxonne: large bluish purple flowers. (A child of *The Czar*). Exceptionally hardy, and resistant to Red Spider infestation. It is recorded that 7,000 blooms were gathered from a quarter acre plot in Ireland during one week of severe frost.

Rawson's *White*: Free flowering. Believed to be an improved form of *Viola odorata alba*.

Queen Charlotte: The soft purple flowers, and the leaves, are sweetly scented. (Can be obtained as seed.)

For the more experienced, or adventurous, the following are available from the specialist nurseries listed at the back of this book.

Parma Violets (Double): 'The sweetest perfume, flowering season the longest, foliage the handsomest of all double violets'. Frame or cloche protection essential in the winter.

Duchesse de Parme: Pale lavender; prolific.

Marie Louise: Lavender mauve; exotic scent.

Swanley White (Comte de Brazza): Pure white, strong scent. Obtained in the 1880's by Cannells Nursery from the Count's garden near Udine in Italy.

The following hardy single scented Violets can be grown in the open throughout the year, or cossetted with frame or cloche protection in the winter.

Mrs. R. Barton (Alassio): White flowers flecked with purple. Stems long enough to cut. Mr. Barton was the foreman of the renowned Windward Violet Nurseries operated by George and Grace Zambra. (see Bibliography).

Clive Groves: Long stemmed purple flowers with a carmine glow.

John Raddenbury: China blue, strong scent. Originated in Australia. Suitable as a cut flower.

Perle Rose: Described by Roy Coombs as 'an eye catching deep coral rose of compact habit; probably the latest of the scented singles to flower.'

Princess of Wales (Princesse de Galles): Royal Horticultural Society Award of Merit 1895. Long stemmed, giant flowered, violet blue. Bred by Armand Millet in 1889. Probably the most famous of all single scented Violets. Susceptible to Red Spider attack, but appropriate cultural techniques should keep these mites under control. Otherwise does well indoors or out.

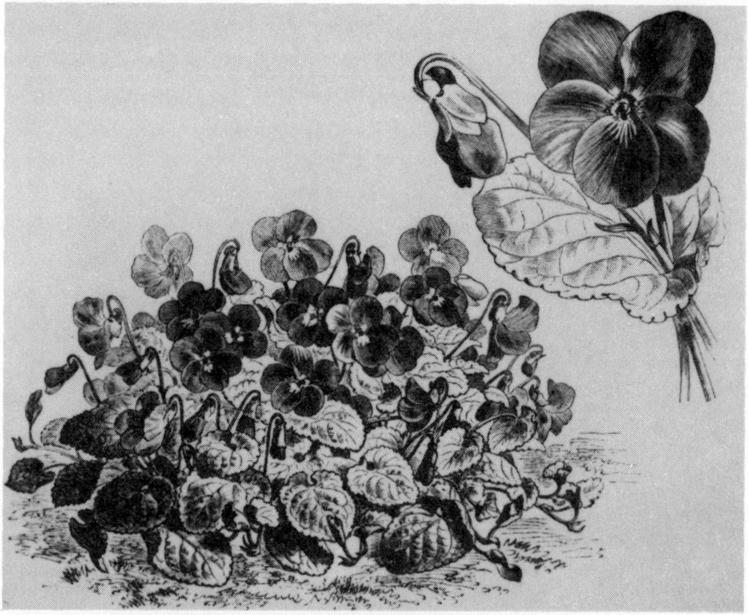

Princess of Wales.

Red Queen: Deep crimson purple. May be a red form of Coeur d'Alsace.

Viola odorata: The native purple or white Violet. Stems too short for cutting, but invaluable ground cover, prospering in the most unlikely spots.

Although the word 'Violet' has become synonymous with scent, most of the species and some of the cultivars are devoid of the merest whiff of perfume. Even in the heyday of the Violet, florists were not averse to sprinkling a pennyworth of Wood Violet from the chemist over a basket of flowers to 'make 'em go.' Today the Violet scent emanating from toiletry products may be of chemical, not floral, origin.

Many of these are beautiful and rewarding plants in the garden, but the introduction from North America in the early 1900's of hybrids between the large flowered single Violets and the robust, but scentless, native species, *Viola cucullata*, almost certainly contributed to the belief that all Violets were losing their scent. The long stems, large flowers and trouble-free physique of Violets such as *Governor Herrick* were an irresistible temptation to many commercial growers, but a salutary warning to the private gardener to select winter flowering varieties that are both Violet by name and Violet in perfume.

Happily the fortunes of the sweet Violet would appear again to be in the ascendant. Clive Groves in Dorset is scouring not only the country but the world, and has recently restored *Mrs. David Lloyd George*, temporarily resident in Australia, to her native land and county. She is flourishing in the company of an encouraging number of other, almost extinct, cultivars, promising an irresistible selection in years to come.

In the open garden Violets, like Violas, are the perfect foil to the smaller bulbs, carpeting the ground throughout the harsh months of the winter and distracting the eye from their slovenly departing foliage in the spring.

Anyone who suspects they may be harbouring an old Violet cultivar would deserve the gratitude of those of us who retain a love for these charming plants if they contacted the N.C.C.P.G. (address at the end of this book) who will put them in touch with the owner of the Reference Collection being lovingly tended in Cornwall.

The purchase of a pot of sweet Violets must be one of the great bargains of the gardener's year. Nurtured with skill and devotion, within a season one tiny plant will have spawned a dynasty, ensuring that names such as *Double Russian*, *St. Helena* and *Lianne* are as familiar to posterity as they were to our grandmothers.

Princess of Prussia.

Pansies and Violets as Cut Flowers

'We hear a good deal of dinner-table decoration, but an earnest effort should be made with the breakfast table as regards flowers... The Briton will never really care about flowers till they come nearer to him - getting the fair forms of many beautiful flowers near the eye is the best way to make converts.' William Robinson (1889).

Painting on silk by Julia F. Gibson.

I had never been entirely satisfied with Pansies as a cut flower until someone pointed out that both flower, bud and leaves must be gathered, the Pansies nestling as naturally in a shallow vase as in the border outside. If a glass vessel is used, moss can take the place of the functional, but unsightly oasis as a support for the stems.

In Victorian times the leisured classes, or rather the leisured wives and daughters of the many successful bankers, industrialists, exporters, importers, railway and shipping tycoons, who chose to reside in sylvan suburbia distanced as far as was practicable from the source of their escalating wealth, discovered in flower arranging a pleasing and acceptable occupation. When hosting luncheon or dinner parties, after the menu had been discussed with cook, there were elaborate table decorations to be ordered or contrived.

Violets were available throughout the winter months. If the gardener was as proficient as his testimonials had implied, these were brought in from frames in the garden. Pyramids of moss were built up in a shallow saucer, the bunched Violets inserted into the damp, springy depths, a trail of ivy artfully arranged to camouflage the receptacle. In the 1860's moss could be bought for 1d. a bundle; nowadays we usually have to gather our own. Refreshed daily, the arrangement lasted several days, especially if removed to a cool room or cellar, or covered with a bell glass, at night.

The winner of the first competition for table decorations, held by the Royal Horticultural Society in 1861, T.C. March, favoured simplicity, submitting that many flowers looked bewildered when married with ornate containers. He was delighted when an old gardener, confronted with the honoured exhibit, complained that 'the flowers might have come out of a ditch.'

Pansies of one colour, or at most two harmonising shades, look best. Bowls of mixed colours tend to parallel the gaudily patterned carpets so beloved of interior decorators when converting a simple village haven into an expensive, jangling public house.

Violets in pots

> *'The culture of the Sweet Violet is so simple, and home-grown flowers of it are so charming, in every way, in the dull months of the year.'* *Dobie's Horticultural Handbook* (1898).

Being confined in pots is a plight Violets most especially dislike, but perhaps it is a fleeting luxury that we can grant ourselves from time to time.

* Tease out divisions in the spring, and over-summer in rich, moist ground in a sunny border.

* Lift and pot up with a large root ball in August.

* Plunge pots in ashes in a shady frame, transferring to a sunny one in October. Ventilate freely.

* Bring in to the conservatory or house as they come into flower.

Alternatively, throughout the summer mound up nutritious compost around selected offsets, potting up in the autumn only those already in bud.

In the days when rolling meadows, browsing cows and leafy woods were within sight of many a garden gate, the preferred potting mix was equal parts loam and leaf mould, some dried cow manure rubbed through a half inch sieve and a generous sprinkling of sand. Today, most will have to make do with a proprietary compost from a plastic bag, hopefully enriched with home-made compost and decayed leaves that have escaped wasteful incineration on autumn bonfires.

An unheated greenhouse or conservatory, or the small glass porches attached to many homes, rarely harbouring anything more stimulating than an old umbrella and a pot of dead geraniums, can be the ideal setting for a collection of fragrant Violets. William Cuthbertson knew that it was worth the effort: 'Those who succeed in getting strong floriferous plants in winter and early spring will be very likely to regard it as one of the most pleasant incidents in their horticultural experience.' Violets over-wintered under these conditions are unlikely to re-adapt to outdoor cultivation, and should be treated as a lovely, but disposable, proposition.

There is an intriguing seventeenth century alternative: 'You may have trees apparrelled with Flowers, or Herbs, by Boring Holes in the Bodies of them, and Putting into them Earth holpen with Mucke, and Setting Seeds, or Slips, of Violets, Strawberries, Wilde-Thyme... Wherein they doe but grow; in one Tree, as they doe in Pots.' [16]

Violets can, of course, be grown simply, and deliciously, as wild flowers:

A Violet by a mossy stone
Half hidden from the eye,
Fair as a star, when only one
Is shining in the sky.
Wordsworth.

Violets by post

'The innumerable gifts that quiet women of the British Isles send to their women friends.' The Misses A. & D. Allen-Brown (1926).

Flowers: Gather early and immerse stems in water for at least two hours before despatch. Don't be niggardly; as with sweet peas, picking encourages a fresh surge of bloom. Secure in single layers. Small flowers travel best with stems swathed in damp moss or cotton wool, the whole bunch enclosed in a sealed plastic bag. Tins with resealable lids make excellent postal containers.

Plants: Despite high postal charges, lift with a generous coating of soil, gently fold up the long roots, swaddle in damp newspaper, kept in place with cling film. Finally, enclose in a stout cardboard box.

In my experience, if the contents are noted on the wrapping the Post Office will make supreme efforts to speed the gift to its destination.

Recipes

'These little Plants are by no means to be excluded a Garden. The fine Blue, or rather Purple, colour, grateful Smell & early Flow'ring in ye Spring make them acceptable as well as recommend them to the notice of most People. Beside their usefulness to the Apothecary some small profit arises to those who gather the Flowers for them to make Syrup of and Conserve,' &c. Peter Aram. (1720s).

Some of us grow vegetables for the table, most of us pick flowers for decoration, but how many of us gather nasturtiums, marigolds, chrysanthemums, heartsease or Violets to beautify our salads, sweeten our drinks, adorn our cakes, scent our puddings, soothe our coughs, ease our aching limbs or comfort our blemishes.

The art of distilling perfumes and liqueurs from flowers, a technique to which many pages are devoted in old recipe books and herbals, is no longer necessary, or perhaps even legal, in today's small private households.

Heartsease has, for centuries, played a dual role, both as a love potion - statistically impossible to evaluate - and as a respected treatment for diseases of the heart.

Publications such as Mrs. Grieve's *A Modern Herbal* specify many medicinal uses, and methods of preparation, for the infusions, compresses and ointments compounded from the leaves and flowers of both the Heartsease and the Violet, these retiring little plants alleviating some of the most feared and painful medical conditions of our time. Many centuries ago, infusions from the Violet were valued 'to moderate anger, to procure sleep and to comfort and strengthen the heart."

A Tudor remedy for sleeplessness was offered by Anthony Ascham, astrologer and Vicar of Burneston in Yorkshire, in *The Little Herball* of 1561. '...for they that may not slepe for sicknesse, [steep] this herb in water, and at even let him soke well hys feete in the water to the ancles, whã he goeth to bed, bind of this herbe to his temples & he shall slepe wel by the Grace of God.'

The seventeenth century herbalist, Nicholas Culpeper, considered that pressing the flowers against the temples was sufficient to revive drooping spirits. However, the Edwardian Anne Pratt observed tartly 'that a great number of Violets, in a small apartment, have, in several instances, caused convulsions.'

Sir Hugh Platt, in his 'pretty volume of experimental observations', *Floraes Paradise* directs the cook to administer to her ingredients in the garden.

> 'Make gum water as strong as for Inke, but make it with Rose-water; then wet any growing flower therewith, about ten of the clocke in a hot Sommers day and when the Sun shineth bright, bending the flower so as you may dip it all over therein & then shake the flower well; or else you may wet the flower with a soft callaver pensill, then strewe the fine searsed powder of double refined sugar upon it: doe this with a little box or searce whose bottome consisteth of an open lawne, and having also a cover on the top; holding a paper under each flower, to receive the suger that falleth by: and in three howers it wil candie or harden upon it; & so you may bid your friends after dinner to a growing banquet.'

A French recipe instructs the cook to 'plant the dish with flowers of Violets and serve forth.'

The method for crystallising flowers has changed not at all since Sir Hugh Platt gave up his recipe in 1608. Gum Arabic (acacia powder) is obtainable from artist's suppliers and some chemists.

> Crush the gum arabic and add sufficient Rosewater (from the chemist) to cover. Leave to dissolve; this may take several days. Gather flowers when dry on a sunny morning. Brush sparingly with gum arabic then lightly dust with castor sugar. Lay on a rack covered in greaseproof paper and place in a warm airing cupboard or low oven, with the door open, to dry. I put mine on a shelf above a wood burning stove, where the wafts of warm air mature them to a silvery crispness within a few hours. Store in an airtight tin.

Violet nosegays are particularly charming. Make a bouquet from half a dozen flowers and a leaf or two, tie round with cotton, then proceed as above.

Jean de La Quintinie, 'Chief director of all the gardens of the French-King', Louis XIV, was partial to Violets as flowers and food. 'The double ones serve to make pretty Borders in our Kitchen- Gardens. Their flowers make a very agreeable Figure when they are artfully placed on the Superficies of Spring-Sallets.' [17]

John Evelyn, officially the translator of La Quintinie's *The Compleat Gard'ner*, rarely overlooked the culinary possibilities furnished by the flowers in his garden, enjoying young Violet leaves fried then dressed with orange juice and sugar, 'one of the most agreeable of all herbacious dishes.'

A delectable twentieth century cookery book, Dorothy Hartley's *Food in England*, today largely ignored in favour of glossy publications where the photographs take precedence over the text, gives an enticing recipe for Violet Ice Cream:

> Fill whipped cream with as much fine fresh brown bread-crumbs as it will carry. Freeze lightly, beat in coarse crystallised sugar, or crushed sugar candy, and chill again. Finally cover lavishly with crystallised Violets. The crumbs must be fine and fresh and brown, and the sugar as coarse as fine crushed ice; the texture is delicious.

Violet tea is made by infusing two teaspoons of leaves to every cup of boiling water. Strain after five minutes, and sweeten with honey. It is said to be very soothing to sufferers from bronchitis.

Only glass, enamel, or pottery utensils should be used in the culinary preparation of flowers.

In the rather unlikely event of a domestic grower being willing to sacrifice large quantities of bloom and leaf, Nelson Coon, in *The Complete Book of Violets* supplies recipes for toilet waters, syrups, tisanes, butters, vinegars, lemonades, wine, soups, puddings; Violets poached, pickled and boiled; Violet jams, Violet jellies, and Violet marmalade.

Pests & diseases

'Foreboding and knowledge of ill creates ill.' The Misses A. & D. Allen-Brown (1926).

In an age seemingly pre-occupied with the hazards and afflictions lurking in wait for the hapless gardener, it might seem churlish to ignore the topic of pests and diseases altogether. However, blessed with an element of luck and a resourceful disposition few, if any, of the following tribulations will affect your own crop of Pansies or Violets.

The Misses Allen-Brown were adamant that 'common sense, cheerfulness and a refusal to be discouraged', were of more value than all insecticides.

Summer or winter, Pansies or Violets, many potential troubles will, quite literally, be nipped in the bud if discoloured, distorted or decaying leaves are regularly removed and burnt. It is worth remembering that healthy, vigorous vegetation is rarely attacked by mischievous insects.

Aphids

Spray with soft soap - 2oz. dissolved in 1 gallon of water, taking care to syringe both sides of the leaves.

Red Spider mite

Perversely, it is rather cheering that this tiny mite has defeated the resources of even the giant chemical companies. Generally regarded as the only formidable pest allied to the culture of Violets, but by no means inevitable; a primary example of prevention being more effective than cure. Symptoms are yellow or mottled foliage, the leaves ultimately exhibiting a scorched appearance. Keen sight, or a hand lens, will distinguish minute creatures, despite their name only red at certain times of the year, and no larger than a grain of pepper, on the underside of the leaves.

Keeping plants moist is the most reliable deterrent. Syringe in the evening, as often as time and energy permit, directing powerful jets of water underneath the leaves.

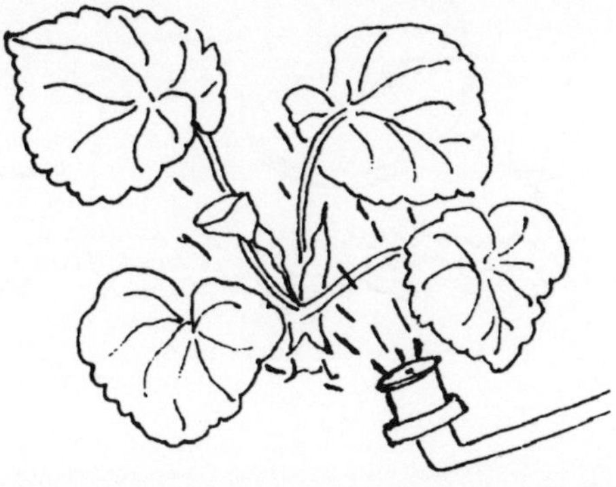

Seaweed extract, available in liquid form from most garden centres, is deemed particularly effective.

Viola *cornuta* 'Perfection', depicted as a disease and pest free bloom that would be a credit to any gardener.

But Violas presented for competition did not always owe their beauty and vigour to the skill of the exhibitor. "We are truly sorry", railed George Glenny in his *Garden Almanac,* "to see gentlemen of spirit, taste, and liberality driven from our public exhibitions by the gross mis-conduct of our floral blacklegs. Will anybody believe that there are amateurs who collect the flowers with which they compete, and beat honest exhibitors ... How would the gentleman who exhibited at Hammersmith, Pansies grown four or five-and-twenty miles from his own garden, (and who pocketed the fruits of his fraud,) like us to print his name, and tell the world who was the worthless, heartless, spiritless trader who supplied him with flowers."

A popular antidote in earlier days during the initial preparation of the bed, and well worth a trial today, was drenching the soil with salt water (1oz. to 1 gallon), followed by a liberal application of well seasoned soot, and sulphur, raked over the surface.

If Red Spider mite persists, strip off and burn all infected leaves, washing the undersides of the remainder with soft soap and water. When dry, dust leaves and soil with weathered soot. Syringe clean three days later. George Lee always set one of his most handy men to the task, 'as it requires some care, that is, that it should be done thoroughly.' A successful nurseryman, he knew that the soot acted both as a deterrent to the pest and a stimulant to the plant.

The supplier of a dispenser for powdered substances is listed at the end of this book. Or use an empty puffer pack, if anyone has mastered the knack of dispersing the contents in the quantity required and in the direction intended. A muslin bag is a cheap home-made alternative. A more recent palliative is Derris. The Red Spider Mite predator, Phytoseiulus persimilis, obtainable from Biological Pest Control suppliers, is only practical under commercial glasshouse conditions.

If drastic action is unavoidable, treat the plants to a nitrogen boost with a quick release organic fertiliser such as dried blood. Although more expensive than the artificial alternatives, Nitrate of Soda and Sulphate of Ammonia, the Violet bed is likely to occupy such a small area that the additional outlay will be negligible.

An old fashioned recipe to cleanse Violets over-wintered in a frame before being planted out in the spring, was brief immersion in a solution of: 1 wineglassful of paraffin, ¼lb. of soft soap, ¼lb. flowers of sulphur combined with 1 gallon of warm water. Quantities can, of course, be reduced if only a few plants are involved.

Tightly curled hard leaves on Violets, not to be confused with the neatly rolled soft juvenile foliage, indicate Midge larvae, and are of no serious concern. Pick off and burn.

Slugs & Snails

> *'It is the early bird that finds the worm - and the early florist may overtake many a bloated snail on his way to his burrow by an inspection of his Pansies at day-break.'* Shirley Hibberd. (1857).

These pests induce a state of apoplexy or despair in gardeners out of all proportion to their admittedly rapacious and villainous behaviour. Anyone who has played host to just one rabbit in the garden would willingly exchange it for a platoon of hungry slugs. Many of us attempt to justify the distribution of poisonous bait or liquids which will inflict as much misery on the helpful as on the harmful. The current tendency to resort to chemicals in preference to exercising the human brain and frame should be resisted.

* Hand picking, accompanied by a bucket of salt water. William Cuthbertson's advice of 1910, that 'slugs must be hunted for at night with a good lamp' cannot be improved upon. Those of a squeamish disposition may use an old spoon or eyebrow tweezers. Slaked lime - exposed to the air in a well ventilated shed - or fine salt can be sprinkled on the smallest or most evasive specimens. Drenching the soil with weak lime water may persuade subterranean slugs to rise to the surface.

* Weathered ashes discourage the more apathetic.

* Small heaps of bran, pieces of carrot or apple secreted beneath a cabbage leaf foster a community spirit, slugs assembling in groups convenient for collection. The nineteenth century florist, Maria Jackson, concluded that slugs actually preferred sliced turnip to growing plants.

* A mixture of soot and lime around plants, and as a thick edging to beds, especially beneath box hedges.

These days one is in receipt of much unsolicited and unsound advice about clearing up the garden. Some orderly souls seem indifferent to the housing needs of the predators who, deprived of an assortment of old slates, bricks, twigs and fallen leaves under which to recuperate in their leisure hours, lack the stamina to keep garden pests under control. Such simple amenities serve the dual purpose of rendezvous points for a number of pests, and should be inspected regularly throughout the year. The number of snails mustering beneath a short length of inverted guttering during the months of hibernation can be truly astonishing.

If more of us remained alert to garden pests throughout the winter, instead of being galvanised into action only after much of the damage has been done, there would be fewer anguished gardeners wailing over damaged crops in mid-summer.

* Pots or cold frames are easily protected by a strip of double sided adhesive tape or a band of petroleum jelly around the rim, on which patrolling slugs are unable to obtain a purchase. The efficacy of a pair of industrious and inquisitive ducks is invariably under-estimated.

Although one can hardly describe the pursuit of the lethargic snail as the lure of the chase, a good harvest will, nonetheless, gild the day with a sense of achievement.

It would be foolish to imply that these methods will effect a total or permanent clearance of a particular problem, but neither will the chemical alternative.

The caterpillars of various nocturnal moths live in the top layer of the soil, emerging at night to gorge on convenient stems. Although hoeing is to be discouraged in, say, an herbacious border which will contain many surface rooting plants, in a bed of deeply rooting Violets and Pansies it can do nothing but good. Grubs will be excavated, to the delight of attendant birds, and Violet runners kept under control with a swift slice from the hoe.

Pest control by birds can hardly be described as free, since they also help themselves to crops one would prefer they left alone. The arrangement is more one of barter, but any profit is undoubtedly on the side of the gardener.

Mildew

1 teaspoon of bicarbonate of soda, 1 teaspoon of soft soap to 1½ pints of water. Spray weekly if necessary, although one treatment is often sufficient.

Pansy sickness

A soil-borne virus which can, occasionally, have a devastating affect on both Pansies and Violas, seemingly healthy plants collapsing overnight. One of our most successful and dedicated growers of Violas and Pansies recommends drenching newly planted stock with a strong solution of 'Benlate'(Benomyl), repeating each month throughout the summer. The Royal Horticultural Society suggests that both seedlings and mature plants should be watered with Cheshunt compound once a week, plus the additional precaution of 4 per cent calomel dust in the holes before planting. If infection should arise - and this is more unlikely than otherwise - the plants should be burnt and new stock located in another area of the garden.

If Pansies are confined to a small area, remove the infected soil, replacing it with virus-free compost, or retain the plants in individual pots sunk into the ground.

Godfrey's Pot Plunger.

The exceptionally unfortunate or neurotic will fret about the real, or potential, damage done by ants, earwigs (which eat greenfly), wire-worms, caterpillars, leather jackets, woodlice, eelworms and fungus diseases of one kind or another. In most instances organic methods of control will reduce or dispose of the nuisance. In the unlikely event of serious infestation, appropriate measures, detailed in publications such as those listed in the bibliography, can be applied.

The hooligan behaviour of some sparrows, fretting at leaves and petals, can be foiled by stringing the beds with black tacking cotton early in the season. Sewing cotton must never be used, as this will not break if a bird becomes entangled in the skeins.

The end

Preparing the gound.

Month by Month.

January

Ventilate **frames** and **cloches** daily, unless experiencing exceptionally bad weather. Pick off and remove dead foliage; keep glass clean. If not already completed, prepare beds for spring planting of **Pansies, Violas** and **Violets.** Transfer potted up **Violas** to cold greenhouse or conservatory. Obtain soot, and put to weather in a dry, airy shed.

February

Frames and **cloches** as for January. Sow **Pansy** and **Violet** seed in gentle heat if insufficient stock available from autumn propagation. Place orders for spring delivery.

March

Harden off **framed plants**, removing sashes altogether by the end of the month. Take runners from framed **Parma Violets.** Watch out for pests and diseases inside and out. Never forget that vigilance has its own reward.

April

Plant out **Pansies** and **Violas** sown in February. Divide all **Violets** at completion of the flowering season. Plant out runners taken from **Parma Violets.** Take cuttings from the fresh young growth of **Pansies** cut back in the autumn. Mulch and feed established **Pansies** and **Violas.** If required, sow temporary shade crop for **Violet bed.**

May

Keep a careful watch over newly planted stock, watering as required. Check for pest damage. Prepare liquid feeds, such as **Comfrey** and **Black Jack.**

June

If required, allow a few **Pansy** blooms to run to seed, otherwise dead head daily if possible. Mulch and feed **Pansies** and **Violets** regularly, applying liquid manure at approximately fortnightly intervals. Syringe **Violets** daily in hot weather, particularly beneath the leaves. Look out for **Red Spider** infestation. Remove runners.

July

Sow winter flowering **Pansies**. Collect **Pansy** seed. Remove lanky, exhausted growths to encourage strong short stems from the centre. Take cuttings for autumn planting. Continue to remove **Violet** runners; mulch, feed, and syringe.

August

Sow **Pansy** seed for next summer's display. Cut back **Violas** selected for division. Encourage and peg down sufficient **Violet** runners to replace mature plants. Prepare frames for **Violets** to be over-wintered under glass.

September

Take cuttings of both **Pansies** and **Violets**. Plant out **Pansy** cuttings taken in the spring. Transfer **Parma Violets** to frames, unless over-wintered under cloches in a south-facing bed. Transplant **winter flowering Pansies**, sown in July, to tubs or window boxes within view of the house.

October

Transfer any hardy **Violets** to be over-wintered in frames. Divide congested **Violas**, potting up a selection for eventual display in a cold greenhouse or conservatory. Plant out **Pansies** sown in August, and cuttings taken in early summer. Detach rooted **Violet** runners. Ensure maximum ventilation for **Violets** in frames.

November

Cut back established **Pansies**. Collect **Violet** seed, if required, otherwise remove capsules. Continue to ventilate **frames** and **cloches**. Prepare **Pansy** and **Violet** beds for spring planting.

December

Have ready mats to cover **Violet** frames overnight in periods of severe frost. Tour the garden with a bucket of salt water on an inspection of likely roosts for hibernating **snails**.

Acknowledgements.

I would like to remember all those gardeners who, through the years, have nurtured, propagated and preserved the ancestors of the Pansies, Violas and Violets that give us so much delight today.

I am indebted to Dr. Brent Elliott and his assistants at the Lindley Library of the Royal Horticultural Society, to Marilyn Ward and the Royal Botanic Gardens, Kew; to Maureen Pemberton and the Bodleian Library, and to the staff of the London Library and the British Library.

My thanks to Sir Thomas Ingilby, Bt., for allowing me to quote so freely from Peter Aram's *A Practical Treatise of Flowers*; also to Macdonald & Company for the use of the recipe from Dorothy Hartley's *Food in England*, and David Higham Associates Ltd., for permission to use an extract from Sir Osbert Sitwell's *Left Hand Right Hand*. Barnicotts of Taunton have kindly granted permission for the use of extracts from the Misses A. and D. Allen-Brown's *The Violet Book*.

I am grateful to Yvonne Mathews and Clive Groves for sparing the time to talk about Violets, proving that all true gardeners can magically salvage calm moments from hectic schedules in which to dwell on the flowers they love. To Graham Pattison of the N.C.C.P.G. for a flow of helpful information; to Julia Gibson, and again to Yvonne Mathews, for their charming paintings, executed at short notice by two very busy women.

My special thanks must go to my husband for his skill, tenacity and patience in assembling and designing the book on his computer, a machine that I continue to distrust but no longer hold in contempt.

Attributions.

1. J. Sinclair and J. Freeman. *A History and Description of the different varieties of the Pansey or Heartsease.*

2. *The Flower Gardener's Library and Floricultural Cabinet*, 1841.

3. Thomas Hogg. *A Practical Treatise.*

4. & 5. As (1).

6. As (2).

7. Gertrude Jekyll. *Wood and Garden.*

8. Jane Loudon. *Botany for Ladies.*

9. *The Garden*, 1887.

10. Francis Bacon. *Sylva Sylvarum.*

11. Peter Aram. *A Practical Treatise of Flowers.*

12. Rev. Prof. G. Henslow. *Botany for Beginners.*

13. E.J. Perfect. *Russian Violets.* R.H.S. Journal, Vol. 90, 1965.

14. *Journal of Horticulture*, 1905.

15. Ibid.

16. As (10).

17. Jean de La Quintinie. *The Compleat Gard'ner.*

Illustrations.

Additional illustrations by the author.

Selected bibliography.

Allen-Brown, A. and Allen-Brown, D. *The Violet Book*. Bodley Head, 1913; Barnicott & Pearce/The Wessex Press, 1924/1926.

Aram Peter. *A Practical Treatise of Flowers*. Ingilby MS 3664 1720's: Ed. Frank Felsenstein. Leeds Philosophical and Literary Society, 1985.

Ascham, Anthony. *The Little Herball*, 1561(?).

Buczacki, Stefan and Harris, Keith. *Pests, Diseases and Disorders of Garden Plants*. Collins, 1981.

Burrows, Jean. *Lee's Legacy*. N.C.C.P.G. Newsletter No. 10, 1987.

Cook, E.T. *Sweet Violets and Pansies*. Country Life and George Newnes, 1903.

Coombs, Roy E. *Violets*. Croom Helm, 1981.

Coon, Nelson. *The Complete Book of Violets*. A.S. Barnes, U.S.A/Thomas Yoseloff, London, 1977.

Crane, D.B. *Pansies and Violets*. Collingbridge 1908.

Cuthbertson, William. *Pansies, Violas and Violets*. Jack, 1910.

Dobie's Horticultural Handbook. *Pansies, Violas and Violets*. 1898.

Estienne, Charles. *Maison Rustique*, or *The Countrey Farme*. Translated by Richard Surflet. Revised and augmented by Gervase Markham, 1616.

Grieve, M. *A Modern Herbal*. Jonathan Cape, 1931.

Hartley, Dorothy. *Food in England*. Macdonald & Co., 1954/Futura paperback, 1985.

La Quintinie, Jean de. *The Compleat Gard'ner*. Translated by John Evelyn. M. Gillyflower, 1693.

Millet, A. *Les Violettes*. O. Doin, Paris, 1898.

Perfect, E.J. *Russian Violets*. Journal of the Royal Horticultural Society, October, 1965.

Simkins, James. *The Pansy: and How to Grow and Show It*. Cornish Bros/Simpkin, Marshall & Co., 1889.

Sinclair, J. and Freeman, J. *A History and description of the different varieties of the Pansey or Heartsease*. Effingham Wilson, 1835.

Temple, Jack. *Gardening Without Chemicals*. Thorsons, 1986.

Zambra, Grace. *Violets for Garden and Market*. Collingbridge 1938. 2nd edtn., 1950.

Useful addresses.

Nurseries specialising in Pansies, Violas, Violettas and Violets.

Richard Cawthorne,
Lower Daltons Nursery,
Swanley Village,
Swanley, Kent. BR8 7NU. (Catalogue).

C.W.Groves & Son,
Groves Dorset Violets,
The Nurseries,
West Bay Road,
Bridport, Dorset. DT6 4BA. (Catalogue).

Hazeldene Nursery,
Dean Street,
East Farleigh,
Maidstone, Kent. (Catalogue).

Elizabeth MacGregor,
Ellenbank,
Tongland Road,
Kirkudbright, DG6 4UU. (Catalogue).

Suppliers.

John Bell & Croyden, (Gum arabic)
54 Wigmore Street,
London W1H OAU.

J.W.Boyce,
Bush Pasture,
Lower Carter Street,
Fordham,
Ely, Cambridgeshire. CB7 5JU. (Catalogue).

Buckingham Nurseries, (Box hedging)
3 Tingewick Road,
Buckingham. MK18 4AE. (Catalogue).

Chase Organics (G.B.) Ltd.,
Addlestone,
Weybridge, Surrey. (Catalogue).

Henry Doubleday Research Association,
National Centre for Organic Gardening,
Ryton-on-Dunsmore, Coventry. CV8 3LG. (Catalogue).

Falkiner Fine Papers Ltd., (Gum arabic in solid form)
76 Southampton Row,
London, W.C.1.

J. Gibbs, Ltd. (Kioritz hand duster)
Lovelace Works,
Ripley, Woking, Surrey. GU23 6AW.

Suttons Seeds,
Hele Road,
Torquay, Devon. TQ2 7QJ. (Catalogue).

Societies.

The Hardy Plant Society,
c/o Mrs Sambrooke,
214 Roxley Lane,
West Ewell, Surrey. KT17 9EU.

National Council for the Conservation of Plants and Gardens, (N.C.C.P.G.)
c/o The Royal Horticultural Society,
Wisley Garden,
Woking, Surrey. GU23 6QB.

National Viola and Pansy Society,
c/o E. Hazleton,
16 George Street,
Handsworth, Birmingham. B21 OEG.

North of England Pansy and Viola Society,
c/o P.B. Atack,
46 Westgate,
Cleckheaton, W. Yorkshire. BD19 HB5.

A list of private gardeners selling Violets in small quantities can be obtained from the publisher on receipt of a stamped self-addressed envelope.

Index

Notes